Annie's Edwardian Cookery Book

Annie's Edwardian Cookery Book

Pelham Books

First published in Great Britain in 1972 by Pelham Books Ltd
52 Bedford Square, London, W.C.1

7207 0197 x

Printed in Great Britain by
Northumberland Press Limited, Gateshead
and bound by James Burn at Esher, Surrey

Contents

Introduction

Dear Readers,

This book of recipes was given to me over twenty years ago by Annie, who had been an assistant cook at Tottenham House, the fine residence of the Marquis of Ailesbury.

When I knew Annie she was a cook at the village school canteen in Great Bedwyn, Wiltshire. The canteen meals could be tasteless and the meat portions meagre in the years just after the 1939-45 World War, but Annie contrived to give them a little more flavour and appeal. I was a teacher at the school and enjoyed many a good talk with Annie on the arts of cooking. As a girl working in the kitchens of this great house, which is situated in beautiful Savernake Forest, Annie copied out these recipes in a clear and copperplate hand. They give a complete and charming glimpse of life in Edwardian England—the ease and luxury 'upstairs' and the hard work and long hours 'downstairs'.

I can hear Annie's shrill voice and rapid tongue now . . . 'Up before six in the morning Mrs Haine and often late to bed at night. Fresh scones and cakes to be made every day for tea; stirring sauces on the big old ranges till the soles of my feet burned; often I've skinned thirty rooks before breakfast ready for a rook pie for dinner; and when the house was full of guests we had to run then I can tell you' . . . and so she talked on and I enjoyed listening. The workers in the house and on the estate were truly 'in service'; they gave much and learned a great deal in return.

Tottenham House is now a boys' preparatory school where the fare is no doubt very different from the recipes in this book, which range from the Cordon Bleu standard of Turban *à la Rossini* to how to cook pig's feet and how to make a bladder of lard. There are dishes *à la* Victoria; *à la* Princess of Wales; Eclairs *à la* Vanderbilt; and Little Soufflés *à la* Marlborough. There are Shrewsbury Cakes too for proud Salopians to enjoy.

The food is good and the most impressive part of it all was the immense amount of trouble and time that the cooks spent on their dishes and that everything was what it said it was. Even an ordinary sandwich was filled with thin slices of gruyère cheese, then a layer of clotted cream then chopped cooked lobster, chopped fresh tarragon and chervil, and filleted anchovies.

There is also a recipe for 'Magic Pain Killer'; whether this is for gout, stomach ache, or the ills that beset us in old age I do not know but remember it's 'Magic'.

And so to, Good Reading, Good Cooking And Good Eating

Joan M. Haine (Mrs)

Brail Farm,
Gt. Bedwyn,
Wiltshire.

Preface

By Bee Nilson

I have very much enjoyed preparing Annie's recipes for publication. They are what I had always imagined cooking would be like in a well-to-do Edwardian household. Since that time, two world wars and food rationing, a slump in between wars, and a shortage of staff trained in good cooking, all have had their effect.

But now that a larger percentage of the population has money to spend on good food and an interest in good cooking it seems to me appropriate that we should take notice of, and learn from, the kind of cooking Annie and her contemporaries did.

Annie uses lots of butter, eggs and cream, fresh fruit in season, things from the sea such as lobsters, shrimps, oysters, whiting and sole; and of course, meat of all kinds and not only the expensive cuts either. She doesn't splash wine into everything, but she carefully seasons all food, including among other things, fresh herbs, and spices such as cloves, ginger, cinnamon and nutmeg. Occasionally she remarks that a little claret or sherry added to a recipe 'is a great improvement'.

When she cooks something simple like stewed pears she flavours them with cloves and then adds lemon juice. When she makes a prune jelly she takes the trouble to crack the prune stones and use the kernels. She makes aspic jelly without stock but clears it with egg whites and it is beautifully seasoned. She tells us how to prepare the lettuce to house a delicate shrimp salad. When she prepares stuffed eggs she leaves the filling feathery and light and doesn't torture and squash it in a piping bag.

This has been fascinating reading for me. All I have done in preparing the recipes has been to put them in alphabetical order within their categories, which are Annie's. Where ingredients and utensils she mentions are no longer in general use, I have added an explanatory footnote in the hope that it will help those using the recipes to select an appropriate modern substitute.

I am indebted to Mrs Haine for asking Annie to explain a few things which puzzled me and this Annie did with precision and clarity.

It is very clear to me that the recipes were written by someone who actually made the dishes and this, in my opinion, is one of the things which makes the book unusual. Many compilers of cookery books of the same period, as well as before and since, have not themselves been cooks, but simply collectors of recipes.

I found it interesting to examine Annie's grouping of the recipes—the dishes considered suitable for breakfast including, brawn, galantine, pig's feet and curry—what constituted an entrée—the great variety of savouries—the evidence that liqueurs were home-made, a gallon at a time—and the comparatively large number of recipes for puddings and sweets.

Some of the recipes are very short and no method is considered necessary, for example, 'Granny's Plum Pudding'. Any cook knows you just mix everything together; but she does tell you how long to cook it. Where recipes are involved and tricky she gives much careful detail not only with quantities, but the precise method of procedure at each step.

While I wouldn't call it a book for beginners, any

moderately experienced cook who is prepared to follow instructions carefully, should have no trouble and will add some delightful recipes to her repertoire.

However experienced you are you are bound to learn something new from Annie.

Breakfast Dishes

Brawn

Remove the tongue and brains from a pig's head and lay all in salt for one day. Drain away the salt and put fresh, taking care that the head is well covered with it, especially about the eyes and ears. In 3 days' time add to the brine 1 tablespoonful of allspice, black pepper and crushed saltpetre. Turn the head well about in the pickle for 3 or 4 days more when it will be sufficiently salted. Boil the head and tongue till tender, then take the meat from the bones and cut it up as hot as you can. The brains should be tied in muslin and boiled for ½ an hour only; break them up and mix with the meat of the head. Season the whole with black pepper and allspice and if necessary add salt. Cut up the tongue, after skinning it, in large pieces and mix with the meat. Have ready a collaring tin,* put in the brawn, set a weight on the top and allow it to stand till the next day. Excellent brawn may be made by using only the eye pieces, ears, tongue and brains of 2 heads, reserving the cheeks for chaps.

Curry

Cut the *cooked* meat into pieces about an inch square. Take about 2 ozs. nice dripping or butter and put into

* A collaring tin was cylindrical in shape and used as an alternative to a brawn-press. Collared meat could be either a piece of meat rolled, tied with string, boiled and then served hot, or pressed to serve cold; or it could be cut up meat, pressed, such as a brawn.

a frying pan with 3 or 4 large onions cut in rings, fry a nice brown. Then put in 2 good tablespoonfuls of curry powder keeping it stirred all the time in the frying pan. Pour about 1 pint good gravy into the frying pan and put salt, vinegar, lemon juice, lemon peel cut fine, and a saltspoonful of sugar to it. Give it a good boil up and pour it over the meat which must be put in a stewpan with about 2 tablespoonfuls of fine white bread-crumbs strewn over it. Let it stand by the fire and simmer for one hour. It is better made the day *before* it is wanted.

Galantine

Salt the rind of a loin of pork for a few days. It must not have on it more than ¼ inch of fat. When required for use soak it to make it roll well, lay it flat and place on it a layer of lean ham, then one of sausage meat or other forcemeat highly seasoned with pepper, salt and sweet herbs mixed into a paste with an egg and ¼ of its weight in bread-crumbs and made very tasty with essence of anchovy; pass a knife twice over a clove of garlic and stir the mixture and if not objected to add a minced shallot. Forcemeat for galantine should always have fat in equal proportions to the lean then it will not eat dry. On the forcemeat put a layer of cooked tongue, pigs or sheep's will do, if you have any pieces of game, fowl or rabbit at your command they make an improvement. Add a few pistachio kernels blanched and mushrooms if they are to be had. On this press another layer of forcemeat as before and then roll all up tightly in the skin. Put it into a cloth and bind it with a broad tape.

Boil it in weak stock or, if you have none, water salted and peppered, an onion or two, some cloves, a little fat or a few bacon bones. It will take from 3 to 4 hours according to the size. When done let it get cool in the liquor, then take it out but do not remove the cloth, place it to press between two dishes and put a heavy weight on the top. Let it remain 24 hours, then remove the cloth, trim the edges and glaze it. Fowls that are too old for roasting make excellent galantine. They should be boned, the meat divided into convenient sized pieces and placed at intervals between the forcemeat.

Kedgeree

Boil a breakfastcupful of rice, strain it. Boil 4 eggs hard. Mince all together with the cold boiled fish. Put a large piece of butter in a stewpan and make the mince very hot. Season with pepper and salt.

Marbled Rabbit

Take two fine rabbits, draw out the livers and kidneys. Steam them tender in a stewpan with a piece of butter. Lay the rabbits to blanch in two or three lukewarm waters. Put them in a stewpan with a bunch of sweet herbs, an onion with 6 cloves stuck in it, salt, pepper and a bay leaf. Pour in cold water enough to cover the rabbits and let them simmer till tender. Cut the meat off the backs and legs in solid pieces. Scrape the rest of the bones and put the bones back to the liquor in the stewpan with ½ oz. gelatine, and after scraping the heads and necks from the meat, let them be added to the other bones and stew till you have a pint of strong gravy. While the bones are stewing lay in a few rashers of ham or bacon to simmer till cooked, then take them out. Mince the scrapings and small pieces of meat very fine with an equal quantity of bacon. Season this with pepper and salt, chopped parsley, thyme and a grate of nutmeg. Bind it with an egg and form little balls. Lay these also in with the bones and cook 10 minutes then take out the balls and strain a little of the gravy into a plain mould that has been dipped in cold water and let it flow round. Place in the pieces of rabbit with balls between them and here and there half a hard boiled egg, a piece of dark coloured liver or kidney, a rasher of ham, or a piece of cooked tongue, not packed too closely, till the mould is full. Season the jelly well and strain into the meat. When it has stood a night scrape off the fat and turn out.

Mock Brawn

Take a fine sheep's head, clean it thoroughly and boil it for five minutes in salt and water. Then put into fresh water with 1 lb. pickled pork and boil both till thoroughly done; the addition of pig's feet or a little of the rind of pork thoroughly cooked is a great improvement. When done carefully take the meat from the head and cut it up with the pork. Mix with the brains and tongue, season the whole with black pepper and allspice, add salt if necessary. Have ready a collaring tin,* put in the brawn,

* A collaring tin was cylindrical in shape and used as an alternative to a brawn-press.

set a weight on the top and allow it to stand till next day.

Pig's Feet

Get the feet of large bacon pigs, boil them gently for 10 or 12 hours or till the bones slip out easily. They should retain their shape and be as tender as a chicken. If the feet have been salted let them soak for 2 or 3 hours, before putting them on to boil, in cold water with an onion, bay leaf and 2 cloves, but if the feet are fresh as they should be, with a little salt. When done divide each down the middle, draw out the long bones and let the feet get cold. Dip each piece in dissolved butter and then in very fine sifted bread-crumbs. Put them on the gridiron* over a slow fire and let them cook until hot through and the crumbs nicely browned turning them both sides. Serve cold.

White Galantine

Bone a fowl, lay it flat on a board, skin downwards, sprinkle it with pepper and salt and a very little sweet herb. Make an omelette of the yolks of 3 eggs and another of the whites, lay the first on the fowl then a layer of fat bacon or ham, then the white omelette and then a layer of ham; over this spread about a 1 lb. highly

* A gridiron was a utensil with iron bars for supporting meat during grilling. It usually had a fairly long handle and sometimes small feet as well.

seasoned forcemeat or sausage meat. A few mushrooms may be added with advantage. Roll up the galantine tightly keeping it round so as to resemble a roll pudding, tie it in a cloth and bind with tape in order to keep the shape. Boil the galantine very slowly for 2 hours in stock. When done let it cool in the liquor. Put the galantine between two dishes, place a weight on the top and let it remain in this press for 12 hours. The tape should be unwound before pressing but the ends must be left securely tied. Take care to put the joins of the cloth on the under side so as to keep the upper side of the galantine smooth. Prepare a pint of good white sauce, it must be thick, with milk and when nearly cold stir in ½ oz. Nelson's gelatine dissolved in a gill of milk. Spread this with a large knife smoothly on the galantine taking care to cover the whole surface; dipping the knife occasionally in boiling water will assist the smooth spreading of the white glaze. Cut pretty shapes of beetroot leaves, flowers, ornament the galantine and dish with these and small sprigs of endive and water cress.

Yorkshire Brawn

Take a pig's head and feet, cleanse them thoroughly, cut the head and ears up, put into a stewpan, cover with water and add a teaspoonful of salt, a good pinch of pepper and chopped sage. Place it on the fire until it boils, then simmer gently till the meat is all off the bones. Take it up and chop it in a hot basin, add all the liquor in which the meat was boiled, stir it up well and put into earthenware jelly moulds. It will not keep long in warm weather.

Cakes

Almond Crescents

Mix ½ lb. of ground almonds with 1 lb. of sifted icing sugar, the yolks of 2 eggs and the juice of ½ a large lemon. Work it into a stiff paste, and roll it out to about ¼ inch thick. Cut the paste into shapes with a crescent-shaped cutter, dust them with sugar, and dry them in a cool oven for some hours on an oiled baking sheet. When they are done and cold, coat them smoothly with icing, made by stirring 8 ozs. of icing sugar with a spoonful of water, and a few drops of rum in a stew-pan on the stove until it is warm.

Breakfast Cakes

Take 3 ozs. butter and rub into 1 lb. flour. Take a small cupful of new milk and ½ German yeast.* Make the milk warm, add 1 oz. butter and mix with the yeast then add to the flour. Let it rise ½ an hour then make into cakes and bake in a hot oven.

Chocolate Sponge Sandwiches

Put 3 eggs into a basin, add 6 ozs. castor sugar and beat 20 minutes, then add the grated rind of ½ a lemon and

* German yeast was fresh compressed yeast first imported from Hamburg about 1850 and then later from Rotterdam via Hull.

4 ozs. flour. Bake on a flat tin lined with paper. When done remove from the paper and spread half the surface with apricot jam, cover with the other half. Beat the whites of 2 eggs till stiff. Melt 3 ozs. chocolate in a saucepan with a little water, mix with it ¼ lb. sugar. When cool stir in the whites of the eggs. Spread the icing over the sandwiches. Cut into any shape liked.

Derby Cakes

Rub ½ lb. butter into 1 lb. flour, add ½ lb. currants, ½ lb. sugar and 1 egg. Mix all well together with about ¼ pint milk. Roll out thin, cut into round cakes and bake in a moderate oven for five minutes.

Gâteau Mocha

4 eggs, 4 ozs. fine flour, 4 ozs. fine sugar, ½ teaspoonful of baking powder. Put the eggs and sugar into a basin and beat over hot water till they are warm, about 10 minutes. Remove the basin to the table and beat for 5 minutes longer, then sift in the flour and baking powder, stir gently. Put it into a plain mould, buttered and dusted over with sugar and bake till ready. Remove from the tin and let it get quite cold. Then cut the cake into 3 divisions making the rounds as even as possible, while the top must be made perfectly level for icing. Coffee Icing: 4 ozs. of fresh butter, 4 ozs. icing sugar, 1 tablespoonful of clear strong coffee. Beat the butter and sugar till it is quite white like cream, add the *cold* coffee very

gradually, a few drops at a time till it is a firm smooth paste. Spread the bottom layer of the cake with some of the icing then spread the second and do likewise, last the top which spread very evenly with a bread knife. Put the remainder of the icing into a forcing bag with a tube and decorate the cake on the top prettily and put it in a cold place for use.

Genoese Cake

Mix ½ lb. flour, ½ lb. sugar, 4 eggs and a small glass of brandy well together. Then add ½ lb. butter merely melted by the side of the fire and when this is thoroughly mixed pour into Yorkshire pudding tins and bake. Spread jam on one half and cover with the other then cut in slices.

German Gingerbread

Take 1½ lbs. honey and melt it in a basin over the fire. Whilst hot stir in 9 ozs. moist sugar,* 6 ozs. sweet almonds cut in slices, 1½ ozs. ground cinnamon, and 3 ozs. candied lemon peel cut fine. Stir these well together and add as much flour as will make it into a stiff paste. Roll it out several times till quite smooth and stiff and about ½ inch or less in thickness. Divide with a sharp knife into cakes, place on buttered tins and bake in a moderate oven till of a pale brown colour.

*Moist sugar is a fine, soft brown sugar (Barbados).

Gingerbread (1)

1 lb. treacle, 1½ lbs. flour, ¼ moist sugar, 1 oz. ground ginger, 2 eggs, 4 ozs. butter, 1 teaspoonful of carbonate of soda and ½ pint milk warmed. Make into a stiff paste and bake it in a tin. It requires longer baking than a common cake. Warm the tin before the paste is put into it, and warm all the ingredients before mixing. Melt the butter in the treacle before the fire.

Gingerbread (2)

1 lb. flour, 1 lb. treacle, ¼ lb. sugar, ¼ lb. raisins, ¼ lb. currants, ¼ lb. butter, 3 teaspoonfuls of ground ginger, ½ a nutmeg grated, 3 eggs and a large dessert-spoonful of baking powder. Line a baking tin with buttered paper, pour in the mixture and bake 1½ hours in a moderate oven.

Gold Cake

Beat ¼ lb. butter with ½ lb. castor sugar till it creams, add the well beaten yolks of 5 eggs, mix with these ½ lb. flour mixed with a few grains of turmeric. Add ¼ teaspoonful of carbonate of soda dissolved with ½ gill of milk, the strained juice of a lemon and the rind of an orange grated, 1 teaspoonful of vinegar and a little ground mace. Butter a cake tin, pour in the batter and bake in a hot oven ¾ hour to an hour. Ice with *Golden*

Icing made as follows: Mix together the strained juice of 1 lemon, 2 tablespoonfuls of water and 2 pinches of turmeric powder and boil in an enamelled saucepan. Pour the boiling water on 1 lb. castor sugar. Mix with a wooden spoon till quite smooth then ice the cake and stand on a sieve to cool. The icing must be hot when used. Cherries, angelica or any other ornaments can decorate the cake.

Hot Cakes for Afternoon Tea

1 lb. flour, 5 ozs. butter, rub till smooth. Add a little salt and enough milk, about 1 pint, to make into a paste. Mix up very lightly and roll out quickly. Stamp out with a round cutter and bake for about 15 minutes in a quick oven. Cut open and butter whilst hot and serve at once.

Jumbles

1 lb. castor sugar, the grated rind of 2 lemons, 1 lb. flour, 4 well beaten eggs and 6 ozs. warm butter. Drop the mixture on buttered tins and bake in a very slow oven. They should be pale but perfectly crisp.

Little Cakes

½ lb. flour, 4 ozs. sugar, 4 ozs. butter, bake them upon tins.

Milk Cakes (Irish)

Rub 3 ozs. lard into ¾ lb. flour, add a pinch of salt and sufficient milk to make into a paste. Roll out and cut into round cakes. Bake in a quick oven. When done cut open and butter.

Milk Rolls

1 lb. self raising flour, 2 ozs. butter and about 1 gill milk to make a little dough. Rub the flour and butter together, add the milk. Make it up into rolls and bake 20 minutes.

Parkerhouse Rolls

Boil 1 pint milk and stir into it 1 heaped tablespoonful of lard and 2 smaller ones of sugar. Let it cool and when milk is warm add flour enough to make a batter as thick as muffin batter. Then stir in a good gill of yeast or 2d. worth of German yeast* and let it rise 6 hours. Then sprinkle some flour on the pastry board, lay the dough on it and sprinkle just enough flour on to roll it out ¾ of an inch thick. *Do not stir or knead it.* Cut out with a round cutter, brush the top of each roll with melted

* German yeast was fresh, compressed yeast. Writers of the period advise the use of an ounce of German yeast to raise 3½ lbs. of flour. The yeast worked best at a fairly low temperature.

The 'good gill of yeast' would be a brew of yeast, sugar and warm water, set aside to start working.

butter then double each roll by folding the two opposite edges together like a turnover. Press the sides a little together, brush the top with melted butter, set to rise in a warm place and when very light, in about 2 hours, bake them 10 or 15 minutes in a moderate oven and serve at once. They should be of a light brown colour.

Scones

2 lbs. flour, ½ pint milk, 2 ozs. dripping, 2 ozs. lard, ½ teaspoonful carbonate of soda, 1 teaspoonful cream of tartar. Mix all well together, cut into round cakes and bake 20 minutes.

Seed Cake

1 lb. butter beaten to a cream, 1 lb. sifted sugar, 1 lb. flour well dried, 8 eggs, yolks and whites beaten separately, caraway seeds to taste. Mix the ingredients and beat all together for one hour.* Put the mixture into a well buttered tin shape and bake in a moderate oven.

Shrewsbury Cakes

Rub well together 1 lb. castor sugar, 1 lb. butter and 1½ lbs. sifted flour. Mix into a paste with ½ gill milk

* Annie says this doesn't have to be beaten continuously for 1 hour but in spells of beating, for 1 hour before baking.

or cream and 1 egg. Let it lie ½ an hour, roll it out and cut into small round cakes. Bake in a moderate oven. Caraway seeds may be added when liked.

Soda Cake

1 lb. flour dried, ½ lb. sugar, ½ lb. currants, 5 ozs. butter, 2 ozs. candied orange or lemon peel and 1 teaspoonful carbonate soda and ¾ pint of milk. Mix and beat well together. Bake in a moderate oven 2¼ hours. It must be beaten up to the last minute before it is put into the oven and the soda must be free from lumps.

Sugar Cakes

Rub ½ lb. butter into 1 lb. flour, add ½ lb. sugar and the grated rind of 1 lemon and 2 eggs well beaten. Roll out thin, cut into round cakes and bake in a gentle oven.

Swiss Roll

Take 2 eggs and their weight in flour, sifted sugar and butter. Cream the butter and sugar, stir in the yolks of the eggs lightly beaten, then the white beaten to a stiff froth and lastly the flour. Mix thoroughly and add a little lemon juice. Grease a Yorkshire pudding tin and pour in the mixture about ½ inch deep. Bake in a hot oven for not more than 7 minutes or it will become too crisp to roll. Strew a sheet of paper with sugar and turn out on this. Spread with jam and quickly roll. If not done whilst very hot it will break in rolling. Ornament with bars of pink and white sugar icing, silver comfits and fruits glacé.

Wakefield Tea Cakes

Take 2 lbs. flour, rub into it 4 ozs. butter. Mix 1d. German yeast* with 1 pint milk, warmed. Add this to the centre of the flour and leave the sponge to rise for 1 hour. Then add 1 egg beaten up with sufficient warm milk to make it warm. Knead the tea cakes well, add any fruit, peel or spice required (previously made warm) and set the dough to rise for two hours. Then make into small cakes, roll out, prick the tops and set on a warm baking sheet covered over to rise for 10 minutes. Bake in a hot oven.

* German yeast was fresh, compressed yeast. Writers of the period advise the use of an ounce of German yeast to raise 3½ lbs. of flour. The yeast worked best at a fairly low temperature.

Creams

Aspic Cream

½ pint liquid aspic jelly, 1 gill thick fresh cream, 1 dessertspoonful tarragon vinegar. Tammy and use when cooking.

Lemon Cream

Grate the rind of a small lemon, squeeze and strain the juice. Mix with it ¾ lb. sifted loaf sugar, 2 wine glassfuls of sherry and ½ pint thick cream. Let it stand an hour, then whip it for 20 minutes and put it into jelly glasses.

Swiss Cream

Boil for 5 minutes a pint of cream with ¼ lb. sugar, a stick of cinnamon and rind of 1 lemon grated. Mix 2½ tablespoonfuls of fine flour with the juice of a very large lemon and some cold cream. When the boiled cream is nearly cold stir it well into the acid cream and flour. Lay macaroons in a glass dish, a few ratafias are an improvement, pour the cream over and let it stand 24 hours before using. Whip some cream and heap on the top, ornament with strips of candied orange peel.

Velvet Cream

A teacupful of sherry, ½ oz. of isinglass* dissolved in an eggcupful of water, sugar to taste and the juice of a large lemon. Strain and when nearly cold add 1 pint thick cream and pour into moulds that have been dipped in cold water.

White Cream

Soak 1 oz. gelatine in 1 gill milk for 1 hour, then stir over the fire till dissolved. Put in a basin 1 pint thick cream and whip till quite stiff, then with a spoon stir in the gelatine, 2 ozs. sugar and 1 teaspoonful of vanilla essence. Pour into a mould and stand till cold.

* Isinglass was a refined form of gelatine made from fish, chiefly the air bladders, but also from bones and skin.

Entrées

Baked Crab

Pick the flesh from a crab also carefully pick the inside and mix all well together with a teaspoonful of vinegar, a little pepper and a piece of butter melted, also a small quantity of made mustard. Clean the shell and put the crab in. Cover with bread-crumbs and bake till nice and brown. Send to table very hot and hand crisp toast with it.

Chaudfroid of Game

Take ¼ pint of velouté sauce and ¼ pint of cream and ½ pint aspic jelly and boil them together till they have reduced ¼ part; whilst cooking, any scum that may rise should be at once removed. Take a plain Charlotte mould and line it smoothly all over with aspic jelly. This is done by pouring a little jelly into the mould and then turn the mould round and round in a basin of chopped ice until it has formed a coating of about ⅛ inch thick over the mould. Cut some truffles and some tongue or ham into thin slices and stamp some out into small rounds about the size of sixpence and the remainder cut into triangles. Arrange the triangles round the bottom of the mould so that the points are turned towards the centre and at the end of each point place one of the small rounds. The tongue and truffle should be arranged alternately. When the bottom is ornamented set the garnish with a little aspic jelly and then ornament the sides by turning the mould on its side on ice and as a small portion of garnish is placed in the mould set at once with aspic. The triangles should be placed all round the *bottom of the side* so that the points turn *upwards* and the rounds arranged as at the bottom. Half way up the mould a row of the rounds should come and at the top row of triangles with the points turned downwards. After setting the garnish with a little aspic line the mould with some of the chaudfroid which should have cooled somewhat before being used. This must be allowed to set and then a ragoût made with ½ lb. cold cooked game, 4 or 5 cooked livers cut in thin slices, one or two mushrooms sliced and some truffles also sliced. Make a sauce by putting ½ pint aspic jelly into a pan with 4 tablespoonfuls of brown sauce, 1 tablespoonful Liebig's Extract of Meat,* a wineglassful of sherry and a pinch of sugar. Cook this sauce till reduced ¼ part then mix the ragoût with it and fill the centre of the mould. Let it remain till firm, then turn it out and ornament the dish with chopped aspic.

Cold Entrée of Crab

Take a plain timbale mould and line it thinly with aspic jelly, ornament it with vegetables that have been boiled and cut into fancy shapes. A few sprigs of chervil also look nice amongst the vegetables. Set all with more aspic. Remove the flesh from a crab, put into a basin, season

* Liebig's Extract of Meat was a thick, concentrated meat paste made from beef. Such pure meat extracts are still obtainable, are usually sold in one pound jars, and though expensive have a very long life even after the jar has been opened. They are very superior to the more universal meat or bouillon cube.

with a little cayenne and coralline pepper, salt if required and a teaspoonful of French and English mustard, a dessertspoonful of anchovy essence, a tablespoonful of tarragon vinegar and a little liquid carmine. Pound all together then rub through a sieve after adding 2 tablespoonfuls of thick cream and 1½ gills of aspic jelly. Pour the mixture into the timbale and leave it until set. Turn it out and garnish with a macedoine of boiled vegetables seasoned with oil, vinegar, pepper, salt and chopped aspic jelly.

Creams of Ham

Take ½ lb. cooked lean ham, 2 large raw tomatoes and 2 peeled shallots. Pound all together till smooth, colour with a few drops carmine and mix with ½ pint thick béchamel sauce in which is dissolved ¼ oz. leaf gelatine. Rub through a hair sieve and pour into little fancy moulds that have been lined with a little red coloured aspic and leave till set. Then turn out and arrange a nice lettuce, cucumber and tomato salad in the centre or a pea salad.

Cucumbers en demi Devil

Cut one or more large cucumbers into 3 inch lengths, remove the seeds and peel, and parboil them for ten minutes in boiling salted water, then drain them on a cloth. Fill the cavities with nicely-seasoned chicken quenelle, and braise them in good stock with slices of bacon, herbs, vegetables, and a few peppercorns. When they are done allow them to cool in their liquor, then drain and cut them into thick slices. Dip them in thick mayonnaise sauce, placing on each one a round piece of truffle. Arrange the slices on a border of aspic, and fill the centre with crisp lettuce, pour a little mayonnaise sauce over them and garnish the top with a bouquet of chervil and chopped truffle.

Cutlets of Foie Gras

Line some cutlet moulds with aspic jelly and garnish them with finely cut pieces of white of egg and truffle, set this with a little more jelly. Then place inside each mould a nice piece of paté de foie gras and fill up the moulds with more jelly. When set, turn out on to a cloth, dish up and garnish in the centre with some financière garnish.* You can obtain the garnish in bottles.

Eggs and Artichokes

Boil the artichokes and remove the leaves and choke. Make them hot in butter, sprinkle with salt and pepper and a few drops of lemon juice. Poach some eggs, trim them neatly and put an egg on each artichoke and place on a round of fried bread. Arrange on a hot dish and pour tomato sauce over all.

* Financière garnish should contain cocks' combs, cocks' kidneys, quenelles (usually chicken), lamb's sweetbreads, mushrooms, olives and truffle.

Entrée of Lobster

Make a batter with ¼ lb. Vienna flour,* 2 eggs and 1½ tablespoonfuls of salad oil. Mix into a smooth batter with rather more than a gill of cold water. Make some clean fat hot in a chip pan or fryer, put 2 or 3 dariole moulds into the grease and let them become quite hot. Then take them out, drain the grease from them and pour a very little batter into them and let it form a thin lining inside the moulds. At once drop the mould as it is lined into the hot grease and with a pointed knife turn the mould round and round till the batter has set. This requires ease as if the grease is too hot the batter will bubble up and leave the mould. When the batter has set remove from the moulds and let the cases remain in the grease till they are a pretty golden colour. Take them out and place on a pastry rack to drain. When cold brush the outsides lightly over with a little white of egg and sprinkle a little lobster coral or coraline pepper over them. When required for serving place them on a tin and heat them in the oven or a screen,† then fill them with a ragoût made as follows: Take some nicely flavoured fish stock which can be made from the shells of the shrimps and lobster and the beards of the oysters which will be used for the ragoût. Fry 1½ ozs. butter and the same quantity of flour together, taking care they do not brown, and pour on to them rather more than ½ pint of the fish stock and stir over the fire till it

* Vienna flour was a fine, white strong flour.

† A screen was a device for roasting, baking and heating foods in front of an open fire or the fire box of a range. It stood on short legs, was enclosed on the back, sides and top but open towards the fire. It was made of metal and the food was heated by a combination of direct heat from the fire and reflected heat from the hot screen.

boils, then add the juice of a lemon, 1 gill of cream and a little cayenne pepper. Wring the sauce through a tammy, then add ½ a medium sized lobster cut in small dice, 2 dessertspoonfuls of chopped shrimps, 1 or 2 truffles cut small, 3 or 4 button mushrooms also cut small and 12 oysters. Mix all together in the sauce. Make quite hot, fill the cases and serve very hot. Ornament the tops with one or two shrimps.

Fried Eggs à la Crème de Fromage

Take some fresh eggs and break each into some clear boiling fat or oil sufficiently to cover them. Turn the eggs about carefully till they are a pretty golden colour, then take up and drain them on a sieve (wire). Cut some round croûtons of bread, fry in clear boiling fat or oil then take up. Arrange one egg on each and cover with cheese cream. Brown over the top with a red hot salamander.* Sprinkle with a little chopped raw parsley and coralline pepper and serve as a second course dish or savoury. *Cheese cream:* Cut up 6 ozs. good mild Cheddar or Gruyère cheese into slices, season with coralline pepper. Add 3 or 4 large tablespoonfuls of thick cream, put into a clean stewpan on the fire and stir till it melts. Then use at once and *brown whilst hot.*

* A salamander was a metal instrument made red-hot in the fire and then held over a food to brown it. The part heated consisted of a thick plate of iron and sometimes there was a stand to hold it. An iron fire shovel made an improvised salamander.

Kidneys and Tomatoes

Cut 3 kidneys in half, remove the skin and core. Cut 6 rather thick slices of raw tomato. Have ready some hot butter mixed with pepper, salt and chopped parsley. Fry 6 croûtons of bread a nice golden colour and keep them hot. Boil or fry the kidneys and slices of tomato, place a slice of tomato on each croûton and on the tomato one of the half kidneys. Pour some of the hot butter over and serve at once.

Little Creams of Lobster à la Victoria

Line some Montmorency moulds* very thinly with aspic jelly and garnish the top of each with little rounds of truffle. Set this garnish with a little more jelly, then fill up the moulds with the following purée: Pound together till smooth 6 ozs. cooked lobster, a tablespoonful Béchamel sauce, a large ripe raw tomato, 4 boned anchovies and a saltspoonful of Liebig's Extract of Meat.† Then mix with 2 gills good light gravy in which 1 oz. pounded spawn has been mixed, or colour with carmine and rather better than ¼ oz. Gelatine. Rub the whole through a fine hair sieve, then mix with it a good

* Montmorency moulds. À *la* Montmorency is the name for savoury dishes, cakes or sweets which contain cherries. They were made either in ornamental border moulds or in decorative individual moulds, the latter being the type used in this recipe.

† Liebig's Extract of Meat was a thick, concentrated meat paste made from beef. Such pure meat extracts are still obtainable, usually sold in one pound jars, and though expensive usually have a very long life even after the jar has been opened. They are very superior to the more universal meat or bouillon cube.

tablespoonful of stiffly whipped cream and use before setting. When the moulds are set, dip them in hot water and turn out and arrange in a circle in an entrée dish. Place in the centre a nice salad made of chopped cucumber or celery shredded and put into cold water till wanted. Then drain and season with salt, chopped eschalot, salad oil and tarragon vinegar. Cold Entrée.

Lobster Creams

Whip ½ pint of cream till stiff, season highly with pepper and salt, also cayenne. Cut up half a lobster into pieces, mix with the cream, put into cases with some coral on the top. It is an improvement to ice it before putting into the paper cases.

Lobster Cutlets

Take a good sized lobster and after removing the shell cut the meat into small dice shaped pieces. Make a sauce by frying 2 ozs. of butter and the same quantity of flour together without letting them become discoloured. In another saucepan put ½ pint milk with a blade of mace and half an eschalot. Let the milk boil for about 5 minutes then pour it by degrees on to the butter and flour and stir it into a smooth thick sauce. Season it with pepper, salt and nutmeg, the latter, if liked. Add a dessertspoonful of spawn which has been pounded with a little butter and stir the sauce till it boils. Add the raw yolk of 3 eggs and stir till the sauce thickens, but it must not boil or it will curdle. Wring through a tammy cloth, add the meat of the lobster and mix well. Set the mixture aside till it is quite cold when it will be ready to shape into cutlets. A dessertspoonful is enough for each cutlet, roll each portion lightly in flour, then cover it entirely with whole beaten egg and lastly with freshly made bread-crumbs. Then shape the cutlet using a palette knife for the purpose, do not turn the cutlet during the process and be very careful not to crack the coating of flour, egg and crumbs. Fry in plenty of hot clear grease for 2 or 3 minutes and to give a finish to the garnish of parsley place the first joint of the small legs of the lobster to each cutlet like a bone. The sauce for the cutlets is made with stock from the shells of the lobster, with a sliced onion, a bunch of herbs, 3 or 4 peppercorns, the juice of half a lemon and a little salt if required. Let this simmer for ½ an hour then strain. Fry 1½ ozs. of butter and the same quantity of flour together, then pour on to them ¾ pint of the fish stock, stir over the fire till it boils, add a little cayenne pepper and ½ gill cream, let it boil 3 or 4 minutes. Strain through a tammy and it is ready for use.

Maccaroni

Take ½ lb. Naples maccaroni* and cook for ½ hour in boiling water seasoned with salt. After having drained the water from it cut it up in lengths about 1½ inches long and put it in a saucepan with a pint of well made Béchamel sauce, 1½ ozs. butter in small pieces, 2 ozs. cooked ham or tongue cut up quite small, and if you have

* Naples maccaroni was a variety with large, thin tubes.

them add 2 or 3 truffles also cut up in small pieces. Make these ingredients thoroughly hot then add ¼ lb. grated Parmesan cheese, bring to the boil and serve on a hot dish in a pile. Garnish with small tomatoes which have been cooked in the oven for a few minutes and pour a little good clear gravy round the dish.

Mantua Macaroni

½ lb. cooked macaroni, 2 lbs. spinach, 3 ozs. grated cheese, 1 gill brown sauce, 2 hard boiled eggs, butter, salt, pepper. Brown bread and butter. Boil the spinach and rub through sieve after draining quite dry. Mix with sauce and season. Thickly butter a deep dish, put in a layer of macaroni, then spinach, then slices of egg, and a good sprinkle of cheese and seasoning. Continue till dish is full, let last layer be of cheese. Put bits of butter on top and bake. Serve with rolls of brown bread and butter.

Noisettes de Mouton à la Forestier

Cut the noisettes from the fillet part of a neck of mutton, and trim them into neat round pieces and sauté them in butter in a sauté pan. Wash, peel, and cook in the same pan a punnet of mushrooms, add two or three tablespoonfuls of brown sauce, pepper, salt, and a spoonful of chopped parsley. Stir round carefully, boil them up once, put them in the centre of the noisettes, pour the sauce round, and garnish with potatoes *à la Parisienne*.

To dress the potatoes, cut them, with a round cutter, into tiny ball shapes, and boil them for five minutes in salted water, strain and steam them for five minutes, after which put them in a sauté pan with 2 ozs. of dissolved butter, and finish cooking them in the oven a nice golden colour; sprinkle them with chopped parsley at the moment of serving.

Ox-tail en Matelote

Cut the tail into pieces, put it into a saucepan and cover it with cold water seasoned with a little salt and bring the water to boiling point. Strain it from the tail, rinse the meat in cold water and dry carefully in a cloth. Put into a stewpan about 2 ozs. of good beef dripping and plenty of sliced vegetables, a bunch of herbs, a few peppercorns, two or three cloves and a blade of mace. Place the tail on the top, cover with a buttered paper and with the cover on fry all together for about ¼ of an hour. Remove the paper and sprinkle a little flour into the pan, add a good ½ pint of thick brown sauce, ½ pint claret and ½ oz. of glaze. Replace the paper and let the tail braise gently for 4 hours. If the sauce reduces add a little more stock. When the meat is quite tender remove from the pan and after pounding the vegetables rub through a fine hair sieve. Rewarm it and then pour over the tail which should be served in a pile. Garnish with braised olives, button mushrooms and braised vegetables cut in shapes.

Savoury Quenelle

Make ½ lb. of veal or chicken into quenelle, work it with cream, and steam it in a border mould, one which has an indented top. Cut 4 or 5 medium sized ripe tomatoes into thick slices and cook them in a buttered sauté pan, covered with a buttered paper, in the oven. Then turn the mould of quenelle on to a dish; arrange the slices of tomato on the top; put nicely seasoned, boiled green peas in the centre, and pour mushroom cream sauce round it. To make the sauce: Peel and scrape the gills from a punnet of white mushrooms, wash and chop them with a few drops of lemon juice. Fry the mushrooms with 1 oz. of butter in a stewpan and when the juice has drawn and again been absorbed, mix in a spoonful of flour and a gill of good stock. Stir until it boils, simmer it 15 minutes, then squeeze it through the tammy; return the sauce to the stewpan to warm, adding a gill of cream, and salt and pepper to taste.

Tomatoes à la Newman

Take some nice ripe tomatoes, cut out the cores, scoop out the seedy part with a small egg spoon and season inside with pepper and salt. Prepare some button onions as follows and fill up the inside of each tomato with them, put them into a buttered sauté pan in the oven for 15 minutes, then take up and mask each opening in each tomato with the following cheese cream. Then dust over the top of the cream with *grated* Gruyère or Cheddar cheese and return the tomatoes to the oven for 5 minutes then arrange them on croûtes of fried bread in a hot entrée dish and place some picked watercress in the centre and serve at once. *Onions for centre of tomatoes:* Peel and blanch some button onions then drain and put them into a well buttered stewpan with some salt and pepper and fry *carefully* for 10 minutes. Then add ¼ pint good light gravy, veal is best, bring to the boil then simmer for about ¾ hour adding a little more gravy if required. When cooked the onions should present a creamy glazed appearance. *Cheese cream:* Put into a stewpan ¼ lb. of good Gruyère or Cheddar cheese cut in thin slices, 4 tablespoonfuls of thick cream and a dust of pepper. Stir over the fire till melted then use.

Turban à la Rossini

Well butter a Trois Frères mould,* sprinkle it over thickly with lobster coral or coralline pepper, alternately with raw chopped parsley. Then fill up the inside by means of a forcing bag and pipe with the following force of whiting: Pound 10 ozs. of scraped raw whiting in a mortar till smooth, then pound 8 ozs. Panard. Mix the fish and panard together, season with salt and pepper and 3 whole eggs. Work into a smooth paste then mix in 3 large tablespoonfuls of cream and pass all through a fine wire sieve and use. For the Panard: ½ pint water, boil with 1 oz. butter and a pinch salt. When boiling mix in 4 tablespoonfuls of fine flour and cook on the stove for 5 minutes, giving an occasional stir while it is

* A Trois Frères mould was created for a celebrated pastry cook of the nineteenth century. It is a border mould with a fairly large hole in the middle and a scroll pattern on the sides.

cooking. When cooked use. Smooth the top of the mould with a hot wet knife, place the mould in a stewpan on a fold of kitchen paper. Surround it with boiling water to about ¾ of its depth and poach the turban for about 35 minutes. Then take it up, turn out on to a dish. Surround it with the following sauce and garnish the centre with a ragoût of cooked lobster, bearded oysters, truffles, button mushrooms and serve at once. Sauce: Put the liquor and beards from the oysters and the bones from the fish into a stewpan with 2 or 3 sliced onions, a bunch of herbs, 6 or 8 black and white peppercorns, a little salt and a tablespoonful of lemon juice. Cover with cold water, bring to the boil, skim and simmer for about ½ an hour. Strain it and mix 1 pint of the liquor with 1½ ozs. of butter fried with 1½ ozs. fine flour. Stir till boiling, wring it through the tammy, reboil and use.

Fish

Croquettes of Fish

Take 6 tablespoonfuls of any cold fish, and 2 tablespoonfuls of finely minced lobster or shrimps (shelled), 1 teaspoonful of very finely minced parsley and 1 eschalot also finely chopped. Make a sauce by frying together for 5 minutes 2 ozs. butter and 2 ozs. flour, boil ½ pint milk with a blade of mace and an eschalot in it for 2 or 3 minutes, then pour the milk on to the butter and flour by degrees, stirring it all the time, and it should be a smooth thick white sauce, season with pepper and salt and a little nutmeg, stir over the fire till the sauce boils, then add the raw yolks of 3 eggs and return the saucepan to the fire but on no account allow it to boil. When thick wring through a tammy cloth and add the fish, parsley etc. When cold and firm divide into small quantities, form into balls, then roll them lightly in a little flour, cover with whole beaten egg and lastly with freshly made white bread-crumbs. Place in a wire basket and fry in plenty of clear hot grease till a pretty golden colour.

Fillets of Whiting à la Mornay

Trim and season the fillets of three nice whitings, fold them over, put them on a buttered fireproof dish. Squeeze a few drops of lemon on each piece, moisten them with a little water from the boiled bones. Cover them with a buttered paper, and cook them for fifteen minutes in a moderate oven. Then pour the liquor into a little well-made sauce. Cover the fish with 2 ozs. of grated Parmesan cheese mixed with a little cream. Pour the sauce round the fish and return the dish to the oven to gratinate. Serve very hot in the same dish.

Fish Pudding

Pound or chop small 1 lb. cold boiled fish freed from bones and skin. Mix lightly with it ½ lb. fine *white* bread-crumbs and 1 teaspoonful essence anchovy and ¼ pint cream and salt and pepper to taste. Also 4 well whisked eggs. Pour the mixture into a mould well buttered and steam 1 hour. Turn out and pour good crea sauce *flavoured* with anchovy round the pudding.

Oyster and Haddock Savoury

Take a medium sized haddock and scrape the flesh from the skin and bones. Rub through a coarse wire sieve, season with cayenne pepper and when you are ready to use it pour a little warmed butter over it to make it into a moist paste. Fry some small round croûtons till a nice golden colour; beard some oysters and season them with a few drops of lemon juice and cayenne pepper. Arrange on the croûtons a layer of haddock mixture, then put an oyster in the centre and entirely cover the oyster with more of the haddock mixture, smoothing it with a hot wet knife. Place on a baking tin and cover with more warm butter over each. Cover with a buttered paper and cook in a moderately hot oven for about 5 minutes. Sprinkle a little coralline pepper over them, place a small sprig of parsley or tarragon on the tops of each and serve as hot as possible.

Shrimp Salad

I pint of shelled shrimps, two tablespoonfuls of good salad oil, half a tablespoonful of vinegar, pepper, a teacupful of mayonnaise sauce, six small round lettuces. Put the shrimps in a basin and pour over them the oil and vinegar and a dust of pepper. Leave them for an hour, or longer, if possible. Next pour half the mayonnaise over them. Wash and trim the lettuces, then carefully cut out the hearts, leaving a cup of the outer leaves. Pull the hearts finely to pieces and mix them with the shrimps. Arrange the cups of lettuces in little glass plates, put a tablespoonful of the shrimp mixture in each, with a little mayonnaise poured over, and sprinkle over it all a little chopped parsley.

Soles à la Russe

Cut and turn a dozen tiny spring carrots into lozenge-shaped pieces. Prepare also the white part of a dozen spring onions and a few pieces of young turnip. Boil them separately in salted water until they are nicely cooked, and then strain them. Place the trimmed sole on a long buttered dish, season it with salt, pepper and lemon juice. Cover it with the prepared vegetable, moisten it with a claret glass of white wine (Graves), and cook the sole in a moderate oven, basting it frequently with the liquor. Sprinkle it with chopped parsley, and serve it in the dish in which it was cooked.

Soufflé of Fish

To make a soufflé large enough for 6 to 8 persons. 9 ozs. fish or 2 good sized whitings freed from all skin and bones. Put into a stewpan 3 ozs. flour, 3¼ ozs. butter and a small teaspoonful of Anchovy Essence. A little cayenne and white pepper, also a little salt and the raw yolks of 4 eggs. Mix all by degrees then add ¾ pint milk. Stir these ingredients over the fire till they boil and as the mixture comes to the boil it must be stirred up very quickly or it will become lumpy. When the sauce has boiled add the *raw* fish slightly chopped and lastly add the whites of 6 eggs whipped to a *stiff* froth. The soufflé tin should be prepared before the soufflé is made, it should be well buttered and a band of very well buttered paper must be fastened round the tin so that it will stand at least 3 inches above the tin. After putting the soufflé into the tin sprinkle some browned crumbs over the top, then place here and there on the crumbs some small pieces of butter. It will take about ¾ hour to bake in a fairly hot oven and after removing the paper a folded napkin should be fastened round the tin and a little finely chopped parsley, which has had all the moisture pressed from it should be sprinkled over the top. Serve at once.

Jellies

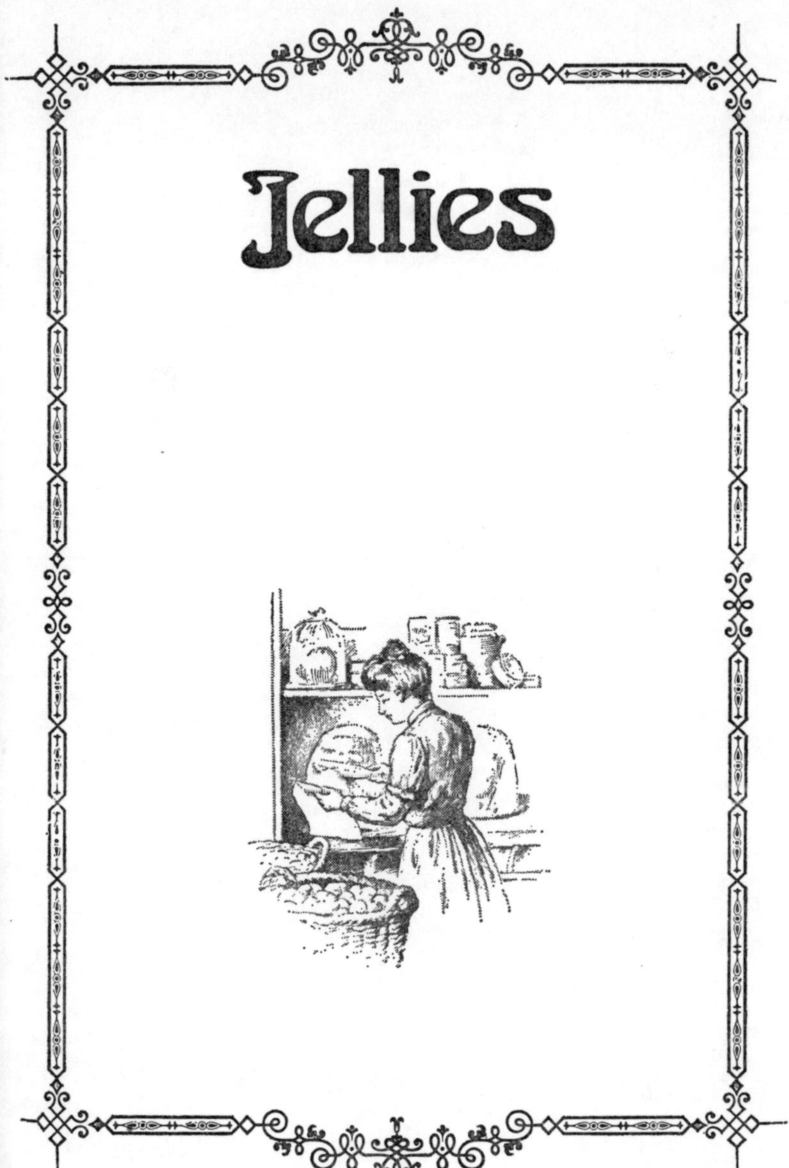

Aspic Jelly

2½ ozs. gelatine, 1 quart hot water, dessertspoonful of salt, juice of 1 lemon, 1 or 2 bay leaves, 2 whites and shells of eggs, 1 small teacupful of common brown vinegar, a sprig or two of green tarragon or 1 tablespoonful tarragon vinegar, 1 onion sliced, and 20 peppercorns and allspice mixed. Mix up all the ingredients and when it comes to the boil, pass through a warm jelly bag. This is made stiff for borders, if required for garnishing use only 2 ozs. of the gelatine for the same quantity of other ingredients.

Gelatine Wine Jelly

Soak 3 ozs. Nelson's gelatine in a teacupful of cold water for 24 hours. Then put it in a brass pan with a tumblerful of brown sherry, a wineglassful of brandy, ¾ lb. loaf sugar, the juice of 2 large lemons and the rind pared very thin. Also the whites of 4 eggs beaten to a stiff froth with a little cold water and the shells broken small. Bring it gently to the boil and then draw it to the side of the fire and let it simmer gently for half an hour. Strain through a flannel jelly bag and pour into moulds that have been dipped in cold water.

Lemon Jelly

For 1 quart jelly peel 4 lemons very thin and cut them in half, squeeze the juice and strain it. Put in a pan with ½ lb. lump sugar, a piece of cinnamon, 4 cloves and about 8 drops of saffron yellow. Take 2 whites of eggs and the shells, whisk and mix with the above. Add 1 quart hot water and 1½ ozs. leaf gelatine. Bring to the boil and pass through a jelly bag till it runs clear. Let it cool a little and then add 1 or 2 wineglasses of liqueur syrup, Noyeau, Maraschino, or Curaçoa, it is ready to use when cool.

Orange Jelly

For a quart mould. Squeeze the juice of 10 or 12 oranges and 3 lemons, strain and sweeten (about ½ lb. sugar). Melt 1½ ozs. leaf gelatine, strain and when rather cool, mix by degrees with the juice and stir well. Then put into the mould.

Prune Jelly

Put 1 lb. prunes into a stewpan with just sufficient water to cover them and the rind of a lemon. Stew gently for about 1½ hours, drain them on a sieve. Take out the stones and blanch the kernels. Dissolve ½ oz. gelatine in ½ pint of cold water, put into a saucepan with 3 ozs. of loaf sugar and juice of the prunes. Boil for 5 minutes.

Colour with carmine, put in the prunes which should be in halves and the kernels. Pour the whole into a mould with a centre pipe or a border mould. When set turn out and fill up the centre with whipped cream. A little claret added is a great improvement.

Liqueurs

Cowslip Wine

To every gallon of water weigh 3 lbs. lump sugar, boil the quantity ½ an hour taking off the scum as it rises. When cool enough put into it a crust of toasted bread dipped in thick yeast, let the liquor ferment 36 hours in a tub then into the cask put for every gallon the juice of 2 and rind of 1 lemon and juice and rind of 1 Seville orange and 1 gallon of Cowslip pips then pour on them the liquor. It must be carefully stirred every day for a week, then to every 5 gallons put a bottle of brandy. Let the cask be close stopped and stand only 6 weeks before you bottle off.

Curaçoa (1)

1 gallon brandy, 5 Seville oranges, 2½ lbs. sugar candy and 2 drachms of cloves. Put it all in a deep stone jar and stir it every day for 6 weeks, then filter through a washleather. The oranges to be put in whole not pricked or speckled but perfect.

Curaçoa (2)

The rind of 4 Seville oranges cut *very* thin, put into a bottle of brandy, let it stand mixed up for about a week or ten days well covered over, then take the peel out and add a syrup made of ¾ lb. lump sugar and a small ½ pint water, add the syrup to the brandy before the syrup is quite cold. These are the proportions for 1 bottle.

Curaçoa (Mother's receipt)

Take the rinds of 8 lemons and 8 Seville oranges, peel *very* thin, 3 lbs. loaf sugar, 6d. worth saffron. Steep 48 hours in a gallon of the best French brandy and strain it off. To be kept a few weeks before drinking it. The sugar must not be crushed or pounded or it will make the liquor thick.

Damson Gin

1 lb. ripe damsons carefully wiped, ¼ lb. sugar candy, 4 cloves, 1 quart gin. Leave airtight for 6 or 12 months, strain and bottle. Do not break the damsons only shake the jar for the first week.

Maraschino

Rinds of 12 Seville oranges and 5 lemons peeled *very* thin. 3 lbs. sugar candy, stir well and then pour over them 1 imperial gallon of gin, keep stirring frequently for 6 days, strain through a napkin and bottle.

Orange Brandy

Take the rinds of 3 lemons and 8 Seville oranges peeled very thin and 3 lbs. loaf sugar or sugar candy. Steep the whole 6 days in 1 imperial gallon of pale brandy, stir frequently. Run through blotting paper or a napkin and bottle off. Cork well.

Raspberry Brandy

Pick fine dry fruit, put into a stone jar and stand the jar in the oven till the juice has run, strain and to every pint add ½ lb. sugar, give one boil and skim. When cold put equal quantities of juice and brandy, shake well and bottle. Some prefer whisky instead of brandy.

Sloe Gin

I gallon of gin, 1 gallon ripe sloes, 3½ lbs. brown sugar candy and 6 cloves. Let it stand 4 months, pour off carefully and bottle. Stir well till the candy is dissolved.

Puddings

Baked Almond Pudding

Take ½ lb. blanched sweet almonds and 1 oz. bitter almonds. Pound them in a mortar with 2 tablespoonfuls orange flour water, 2 tablespoonfuls rose-water, 4 oz. grated Naples biscuits* and ¼ lb. warm butter. Beat 8 whole eggs and mix with them 1 quart boiled cream, a little pineapple essence and ¼ lb. castor sugar. Mix this well with the almonds, etc. Line a pie dish with puff paste, pour in the ingredients and bake till a good golden colour. Serve hot or cold.

Boiled Lemon Pudding

2 eggs, their weight in butter, sugar and flour. Beat the butter to a cream, then add slowly the flour and sugar, beating all the time. Add the well whisked eggs and the grated rind of 3 lemons and juice of 1 (or a large tablespoonful of orange marmalade) and lastly just before cooking add as much carbonate of soda as will cover a 3d. bit, moisten with a little water. Tie tightly down with buttered paper on the top and steam 4 hours. Serve with melted butter sauce round or with sugar syrup flavoured with lemon or marmalade.

* Naples biscuits are made with a sponge mixture and similar in shape to sponge fingers.

Boston Apple Pudding

Peel 1½ dozen apples, core and cut them up small. Put them in a stewpan with a little water, 2 cloves, a bit of cinnamon, and the peel of a lemon. Stew over the fire till quite soft, then sweeten with sugar and pass through a sieve. Add the yolks of 4 eggs and 1 white, the grated rind and juice of a lemon, ¼ lb. butter and ½ a nutmeg. Beat all well together. Line a pie dish with puff paste, put in the mixture and bake ½ an hour.

Cheese Pudding

Melt 2 ozs. butter then stir in 2 tablespoonfuls of flour. Add ½ pint cream or milk, 10 ozs. grated cheese and 6 eggs well beaten. Line a soufflé tin with buttered paper and bake ½ an hour in a quick oven.

Chocolate Pudding

Put ¼ lb. chocolate and ¼ lb. ginger biscuits crumbled into a saucepan with ½ pint milk. Boil all together till they leave the sides of the saucepan. Let it cool, add 3 ozs. sugar, the yolks of three eggs, whip the whites to a stiff froth and add them. Pour into a well buttered border mould and steam 1½ hours. Whip some cream, flavour with vanilla and sweeten with sugar and put in the centre.

Collingwood Pudding

¼ lb. bread-crumbs, ¼ lb. chopped suet, ¼ lb. of jam (raspberry is best), a small teaspoonful of carbonate of soda. Mix all together with one egg and a little milk. Steam for 2 hours. Pour raspberry sauce round.

Crumb Pudding

Take a cupful of fine white bread-crumbs, 1 pint milk, 3 eggs, sugar to taste and either a little grated lemon peel or a few drops of vanilla. Beat all well together, pour into a well buttered dish or soufflé mould and bake. Turn out and pour apricot jam *round* and stiffly whipped cream *over* the pudding. May be eaten either hot or cold.

Fig Pudding

½ lb. bread-crumbs, ½ lb. chopped suet, ½ lb. castor sugar, 1 oz. candied lemon peel cut fine, ¾ lb. figs chopped fine. Beat 5 eggs well, mix all together. Butter a basin, pour in the mixture, tie down and boil or steam 4 hours. Serve with wine sauce.

Gingerbread Pudding

One teaspoonful of ground ginger mixed in ½ lb. flour, ½ lb. suet chopped, ½ lb. treacle, 1 egg. Butter basin and sift a little brown sugar in before putting in the pudding. Warm the treacle and mix in the other ingredients. Boil 3 hours.

Granny's Plum Pudding

1 lb. suet, 1 lb. bread-crumbs, 1½ lbs. raisins, 1½ lbs. currants, 1 lb. sugar, 2 ozs. lemon, 2 ozs. orange, 2 ozs. citron, 6 eggs. Boil 6 hours.

Hot Pudding

Put into a stewpan ½ pint new milk, 2 ozs. castor sugar and a split vanilla pod and bring the milk to the boil. Then add 2 ozs. crème de riz* which has been mixed with 2 tablespoonfuls of cold milk. Stir the mixture till it boils, then let it cook for a few minutes, turn into a basin and let it remain till cool. Mix into it 2 ozs. warmed butter, 1 oz. of macaroon crumbs, the finely chopped rind of a lemon and the raw yolks of 3 eggs. The whites of the eggs must be added when beaten to a stiff froth. Pour the mixture into a timbale mould which has been well buttered and sprinkled with shredded almonds. Place the mould in a stewpan which has

* Crème de riz—rice flour.

enough boiling water in it to come three parts of the way up the mould, watch the water reboil, then draw the pan to the side of the stove and let the pudding steam for 1½ hours. When cooked turn the pudding out and serve with a compôte of cherries iced. The compôte of cherries is made by taking ½ lb. glacé cherries, put them into a stewpan with ½ pint claret, ½ small pot red currant jelly, the rind of 1 lemon cut very thinly so that there is no white pulp on it, a piece of cinnamon an inch long and 2 ozs. castor sugar. Let these ingredients boil until reduced to half the quantity, then remove the lemon rind and cinnamon and colour the syrup with a little carmine or cochineal. Set on ice till quite cold and just before serving add 1 wineglassful of liqueur: Kirsch or Maraschino is best.

Kendal Pudding

Line a small dish with puff paste and lightly bake it. Fill it with sponge cake cut in slices and preserve in layers, pour rich custard over it and stand 6 or 8 hours. Put whipped cream on the top.

Lemon Pudding

3 yolks and 1½ whites of eggs, the juice of 1 lemon and rind of 1 grated, 2 ozs. butter melted and 1 oz. sugar. Lay puff paste round the dish. Grate 1 sponge cake *or* 2 biscuits *or* 2 ozs. ground almonds and mix with mixture. Pour into the pie dish and bake ½ an hour.

Mousseline Pudding

Beat the yolks of 4 eggs well, add ½ pint cream and ¼ pint milk in which 6 lumps of sugar have been boiled and the grated rind of a lemon. Butter some little moulds, sprinkle them with chopped pistachio nuts, fill with the mixture and steam till firm. Turn out and pour round a sauce made of plain syrup flavoured with lemon juice.

Mrs Eyre's Pudding

¼ lb. castor sugar, ¼ lb. butter, beat together to a cream. 4 eggs well beaten, ¼ lb. flour. Mix all together, add a little candied citron cut small and bake in a mould. Turn out and serve with wine sauce or if preferred a cherry sauce may be substituted.

Mrs Gordon's Pudding

1 pint cream, yolks of 8 eggs and a glass of brandy, sugar to taste. Rub the sugar on a lemon. Boil the cream and strain through a fine sieve, stir till cold. Then add the yolks of the eggs beaten and the brandy. Prepare the mould before the pudding is made. Boil some sugar till it is brown, take a warm dry mould (plain is best) and spread the sugar quickly all over inside. When cold pour the custard in and well cover it with paper. Steam it for ¾ of an hour. When cold turn it out. It should be made the day before it is wanted.

Orleans Pudding

2 eggs, 1½ ozs. sugar, ¼ lb. marmalade, 3½ ozs. butter, 3½ ozs. flour, ¼ teaspoonful carbonate of soda. Beat the butter and sugar to a cream, add the yolks, marmalade and flour, then the whites whipped to stiff froth and lastly the carbonate of soda which must be dissolved in one teaspoonful of milk. Pour into a buttered mould and steam 1¾ hours. Serve with arrowroot sauce flavoured with a little marmalade, or you may put a thick syrup flavoured with orange.

Plum Pudding

½ lb. currants, ½ lb. raisins, ½ lb. flour, ½ lb. suet, ½ lb. sugar, 4 ozs. citron, 4 ozs. lemon, 4 ozs. orange peel and large wineglassful of brandy. Carefully pick over the currants, cut each raisin in half, chop the suet and candied peel fine. Whisk well 5 eggs and mix all well together. Boil 8 hours.

Pudding à la Concorde

6 ozs. finely minced suet, 4 ozs. apricot jam, 3 ozs. candied cherries, 3 ozs. sugar, grated rind of an orange, 1 glass of sherry, 4 ozs. flour, 2 ozs. minced apples, 3 ozs. mixed peel, 3 small eggs, ½ teaspoonful cinnamon, ¼ pint of cream or milk. Put all the dry ingredients into a basin, beat up the eggs, add the cream and wine

and with this mix the pudding. Butter a fancy mould and dust with sugar. Put in the mixture, cover with buttered paper and stand in a pan of boiling water allowing the water to come within an inch of the top of the mould and steam gently 3 hours. Serve with German egg sauce or custard sauce flavoured with vanilla, or any pretty coloured fruit purée.

Saxon Pudding

Take ¼ lb. ground sweet almonds and 6 ozs. of Genoise cake (or Castle pudding). Pour over them ½ pint boiling cream and steep the cake until it is into a pulp. Work ¼ lb. of butter to a cream, mix with it 4 ozs. castor sugar and 4 raw yolks of eggs that have been stirred until like cream, the chopped peel of a lemon, 2 ozs. dried pineapple cut up small, and a saltspoonful of vanilla essence. Mix them with the cake and almonds and 2 ozs. crème de riz.* Then whip stiffly the whites of the eggs and add to the other ingredients. Take a plain mould that is buttered and papered with a buttered paper, ornament it in any pretty design with candied peel, cherries, preserved fruits etc. Pour the mixture into the mould and steam it for 1½ hours. Turn it out on to a hot dish and serve with apricot sauce as follows: ½ pot of apricot jam, 2 tablespoonfuls of water, boil for 10 minutes then pass through a tammy or sieve. Add a little carmine and a wineglassful of Maraschino or Noyeau Syrup and use. Serve as a hot sweet for luncheon or dinner.

* Crème de riz—rice flour.

Transparent Pudding

Whisk 8 eggs till quite light, then put them into a clean saucepan with ½ lb. castor sugar, ½ lb. fresh butter, some grated lemon rind and a little of the juice, or any other flavouring. Stir this mixture over the fire till it thickens then let it cool. Ornament some *well buttered* dariole moulds with chopped pistachio nuts, pour in the mixture and steam for 15 to 20 minutes. Serve with syrup flavoured with lemon juice and grated peel.

Preserves

Marmalade (Mrs Stroud's)

12 Seville oranges, 6 quarts water, 10 lbs. loaf sugar. Cut the peel of the oranges up very finely and put into the water with the oranges also cut up. Soak for 24 hours. Then boil for *three* hours, add the sugar and boil rather fast for another hour. Squeeze the juice of three lemons with it when done.

Rhubarb Preserve

To 1 lb. rhubarb put 1 lb. sugar and to every 6 lbs. rhubarb add 2 ozs. sweet almonds blanched and cut into about 3 pieces and the juice and rind of a lemon. The almonds should be added when the fruit is half done. Boil till very soft. Ground ginger and candied lemon peel can be added instead of the almonds if liked.

To Preserve Strawberries Whole

Take equal weights fruit and double refined sugar;* lay the fruit in a large dish and sprinkle half the sugar, in fine powder over; next day make a thin syrup with the remainder of the sugar and 1 pint red currant juice to every pound of strawberries. In this simmer them.

* Double refined sugar—a term used for an old method of refining to produce white loaf sugar.

Sauces and Pickles

Apple Pickle

Boil 2 quarts grated apple in 1 quart of vinegar. Mix 1 lb. onions, 2 lbs. raisins, ¾ lb. salt, ¼ lb. dry mustard, 2 lbs. brown sugar, 2 ozs. pepper (white) with 1 pint cold vinegar. Add to the apple and hot vinegar. If agreeable add ¼ oz. cayenne. Put into a jar and keep in a warm dry place and stir constantly for some weeks.

Chocolate Pudding Sauce

½ pint of water, 3 ozs. icing sugar, 3 ozs. vanilla chocolate cut up finely. Bring the water to boiling point, add a little coffee brown colouring (Marshall's) if liked, boil the sauce for 5 minutes, then wring through a tammy or fine hair sieve. Can be used either hot or cold but if the latter add ¼ pint stiffly whipped cream when quite cold and just beforc serving.

Chutney

Tomatoes 1 lb. Raisins 4 ozs. Powdered ginger 4 ozs. Brown sugar 4 ozs. Garlic ½ oz. Shallots 1 oz. Apples pared and cored 4 ozs. Chillies 2 ozs. Salt 4 ozs. Pound the raisins, chillies, shallots and garlic separately. Break up the tomatoes and mix the whole together. Put into a jar and add 2 quarts vinegar. Place the jar, covered over on the stove and let the pickle remain a month at a moderate heat stirring it every day. Strain off and bottle the liquor for use with fish etc. Then put the sediment, which is the chutney, which must be drained dry, into bottles.

Cream Sauce for Fish

Put into a saucepan 2 raw yolks of eggs, 3 tablespoonfuls of cream, 2 tablespoonfuls of velouté sauce, ½ oz. butter, a pinch of salt and coralline pepper and eight drops lemon juice. Stir and cook in a double saucepan till like cream. For turbot, cod, halibut or sole.

Curing Yorkshire Hams

Sprinkle the ham with salt. Let it drain. Make a pickle of 1 quart strong beer, ½ lb. treacle, 1 oz. coriander seeds, 2 ozs. Juniper berries, 1 oz. pepper, 1 oz. allspice, 1 oz. saltpetre, ½ oz. salprunella, a handful of common salt and a head of shallot, all pounded or cut fine. Boil them all together for a few minutes and pour them over the ham. This quantity is for a ham of 10 lbs.

Dutch Sauce

1 tablespoonful essence of anchovy, 1 tablespoonful of cold spring water, 1 tablespoonful of vinegar and the white of an egg beat up, 2 ozs. butter. Warm the whole until it is as thick as cream stirring constantly.

Fish Sauce

½ pint of good cream, 2 spoonfuls of mushroom Catsup, 1 spoonful of anchovy essence. Boil these together and just before taking off the fire add a little butter rubbed in flour. Stir it all the time.

Horseradish Sauce

1 teaspoonful of made mustard, 1 tablespoonful of vinegar, 3 tablespoonfuls of whipped cream and a little salt, 3 tablespoonfuls of grated horseradish.

Lobster Sauce

Take a fresh hen lobster, split the tail and take out the coral. Pound half of it with 1 oz. butter and rub through a sieve. Cut the flesh into small pieces. Have ready some good white sauce made as follows: A gill of cream, and a gill of good savoury veal stock mixed together and seasoned with cayenne pepper, salt and a little mace. Thicken this with 2 ozs. butter and a dessertspoonful of flour. Let it boil 5 minutes then add the lobster and pounded coral. Make hot and serve.

Mayonnaise Sauce

Mix 2 pinches of salt and a good pinch of *dry* mustard with the yolks of 2 raw eggs then work in vigorously with a wooden spoon drop by drop 4 tablespoonfuls of fine salad oil. When worked enough it should be as thick as Devonshire cream. Mix 1 teaspoonful of tarragon vinegar and 1 oz. chilli with the same quantity of French vinegar. Work this in drop by drop till the sauce assumes a rich creamy appearance. It should thickly coat a spoon and is improved by being placed on ice for an hour or two.

Moti Sauce for Fish

Melt 1 oz. butter in a stewpan, stir in one tablespoonful of flour, and ¼ pint cream. Let it boil, then add 1 teaspoonful of anchovy essence, one teaspoonful of chilli vinegar, a little cayenne. Serve with fried soles or whiting.

Mrs Parry's Sauce

½ oz. cayenne, 1 quart vinegar, 2 tablespoonfuls mushroom catsup, 2 tablespoonfuls of soy, 3 cloves of garlic, 6 shallots and 6 or 8 anchovies. Pound the shallots, garlic and anchovies, mix well with the other ingredients and keep 3 weeks before using it.

Mushroom Ketchup

Take a stewpan full of large flap mushrooms and the skins and fringe of any you have used; throw a handful of salt among them and set them by a slow fire; strain the liquor add to it 4 ozs. shallots, 2 cloves of garlic, a good deal of pepper, ginger, mace, cloves and a few bay leaves; boil and skin well. When cold cork close. In 2 months boil up again with a little fresh spice and a stick of horseradish, it will then keep a year.

Prince Alfred's Sauce

Vinegar 1½ pints, India soy* ½ pint, water ½ pint, walnut catsup ½ pint, chillies 1 oz., shallots 2 ozs., burnt sugar† 1 oz., salt 2 ozs. Bruise the shallots and boil the whole for 10 minutes. Let it stand till cold, strain and bottle.

St John's College Brawn Sauce

Mix 1 tablespoonful of mustard with ½ tablespoonful of moist sugar,‡ 2 tablespoonfuls of salad oil and 4 tablespoonfuls of vinegar.

* India soy was soy sauce made in China and Japan and imported to Britain via India.
† Burnt sugar is caramel.
‡ Moist sugar is fine, soft brown sugar (Barbados).

To Cure Tongues

Wash 6 ox tongues in water, dry them, lay them in a tray. Take 2 small basins of common salt and rub it well all over them. Turn them daily and throw the brine and salt over them. In a week pour the brine off them and put them in a clean dry tray and rub 4 ozs. saltpetre, 6 ozs. soft sugar and a large proportion of salt well into them in every part. Turn them daily, washing the brine over them for a fortnight then dry them with a coarse cloth. Dredge flour over them and hang them up.

Savouries

Anchovy and Lax Savoury

Rub ¾ oz. butter into 2 ozs. flour till quite smooth then add 1 teaspoonful anchovy essence, a little carmine, cayenne pepper and ½ an egg. Mix together and moisten with a little cold water. Roll out very thinly and line some boat shaped moulds which have been lightly buttered. Prick the paste all over and trim the edges neatly. Put a piece of buttered paper in each and fill it with rice, bake for 20 minutes. Then remove the paper and rice and return the tins to the oven to dry the paste at the bottom. When cooked remove from the tins and leave till cold. Partly fill them with hard boiled egg rubbed through a sieve and on this arrange capers, 1 or 2 rolls of lax,* a little crisp salad and an olive which has had the seed removed and is stuffed with anchovies. Arrange on a dish paper in a circle slightly overlapping each other.

Bonnes Bouches à la Moutoise

Take ½ pint whipped aspic jelly and mix with it ½ pint stiffly whipped cream, 2 ozs. grated Parmesan cheese, 2 ozs. grated Gruyère cheese, a teaspoonful French mustard, a teaspoonful mixed English mustard, stir together till smooth. Then put into some little Montmorency

* Lax was canned smoked salmon cutlets preserved in oil and imported from Norway.

moulds.* Put these aside till set, then dip into hot water. Turn out the bouches, sprinkle them with chopped raw green parsley and by means of a forcing bag with a small rose pipe force out a little whipped cream in the centre of each. Sprinkle them with coralline pepper, arrange on a dish paper and use for a savoury.

Bonnes Bouches à la Sauté

Pound in a mortar ½ pint shrimps, 2 anchovies, the yolks of 2 hard boiled eggs, 2 ozs. butter, add salt if required, coralline pepper and carmine to colour a nice pink. Rub through a sieve, then take a nice brown loaf, cut slices as for sandwiches. Spread on the mixture and cut into pieces 3 inches long and 1 inch wide. Decorate the sandwiches with a row of *green* butter down the centre by means of a rose pipe and by discs round and fill the centre with finely picked watercress.

Caviare à la Grand Hotel

Put some caviare into one division of a luncheon tray, into another put a lemon cut into quarters, into a third division put an onion *very* finely chopped (white part only). Hand hot thin crisp dry toast with it.

* Montmorency moulds. À *la* Montmorency is the name for savoury dishes, cakes and sweets which contain cherries. They were often made either in ornamental border moulds or in decorative individual moulds, the latter being the type used in this recipe.

Cheese Straws

¼ lb. flour, 3 ozs. grated cheese, a pinch of salt and a very little cayenne pepper. Mix into a paste with the yolk of an egg. Roll out to the thickness of a shilling, about 4 or 5 inches long. Cut into strips the third of an inch wide, twist them and lay them on a baking sheet, lightly floured. Bake in a moderate oven till crisp.

Crawford Sandwiches

Take a tin loaf, cut some thin slices and spread with anchovy butter. Stamp out with a plain round cutter. Then make a custard with the yolks of 3 eggs, a little milk and some pepper and salt. Beat well together and steam in a plain round mould. When done, turn out and when cold cut thin slices and stamp out with the same round cutter as the bread. Place a round of custard on a round of bread and another round of bread on the top. Serve cold.

Croûtes à la Madison

Take some stale bread and cut from it small rounds 1½ inches in diameter and ¼ inch thick. Fry them in butter till a very pale golden colour, then set them aside till cold. Spread them with a layer of caviare and by means of a forcing bag and large rose pipe force out into the centre of each a little rose shape of Montpellier butter and one of anchovy butter. Arrange each croûton on a separate plate on small plate papers and serve one to each person as an hors d'oeuvre or savoury for dinner. *Montpellier Butter:* Blanch together 3 or 4 sprigs of fresh tarragon, chervil, parsley and fennel with 1 shallot. Strain and dry this. Add 2 hard boiled yolks of eggs, 6 fillets of anchovies, a teaspoonful of capers, 2 gherkins, a little coralline pepper, 1 tablespoonful of salad oil, ¼ lb. fresh butter, a little salt and a little of Marshall's Apple Green. Pound all together and pass through a hair sieve. Mix up and use. *Anchovy Butter:* Take ¼ lb. fresh butter, 6 fillets of anchovies, 2 hard boiled yolks of eggs, a little coralline pepper and a few drops of carmine. Pound all together, then rub through a hair sieve, mix up and use.

Croûtes à la Mariner

Fry a number of pieces of bread a golden colour in butter and keep them warm. Pound the flesh of a whiting with half its weight in smoked haddock, adding 2 tablespoonfuls of good white sauce, the yolks of 2 eggs, a pinch of cayenne pepper, and pepper and salt to taste. Rub the fish through a hair sieve and work it in a basin with a little thick cream. Arrange the cream on the fried croûtes, bringing it to a point with a knife dipped in hot water; sprinkle them with coralline pepper and bake them 10 minutes in a moderate oven. The croûtes must not be allowed to acquire any colour. Serve them on a napkin garnished with fried parsley.

Croûtes of Luxette à la Pompadour

Cut some rounds of bread from a stale loaf and fry till a nice golden colour. When cold spread on each croûton a layer of luxette,* sprinkle on it some capers and place on this a layer of hard boiled yolk of egg that has been rubbed through a wire sieve. Put in the centre a little raw chopped green parsley and arrange on a dish paper on a dish. Use for a savoury for dinner or for hors d'oeuvre.

Croûtons à l'Appetit Sild

Cut some rounds of bread about ¼ inch thick and 2 inches in diameter from a stale loaf. Fry till a pretty golden colour. Brush over with warm glaze, dust with coralline pepper. Prepare a purée as follows: Pound together till smooth ¼ lb. of chicken with 2 ozs. butter, salt and coralline pepper to taste. 1 oz. grated Parmesan cheese, 1 tablespoonful thick cream, 2 hard boiled yolks of eggs, 2 ozs. lean cooked ham or tongue. Rub it through a fine hair sieve and with a forcing bag and large rose pipe form a border with it on the croûtons. Place in the centre of the croûtons one of the prepared appetit sild† rolled up. Fill up the inside of this with a little hard boiled yolk of egg that has been rubbed

* Annie says luxette 'came in a bottle like anchovy sauce—it was very thick and light brown in colour and we never used much of it at a time.'

The Army and Navy catalogue of 1907 lists it as 'Luxette. Marshall's Terrine, 1/- a jar.'

† Appetit sild were canned, smoked sild.

through a wire sieve and on it place 2 or 3 large French capers. Sprinkle on the purée a little lobster coral or coralline pepper and a little chopped raw green parsley and a strip of French gherkin. Then arrange the croûtons on a dish paper. They can be used for a savoury or for hors d'oeuvre.

Croûtons à la Ceylon

Stamp out some rounds of bread about ¼ inch thick and 2 inches wide and fry them in butter till a nice golden colour then set them aside till cold. Then mask each by means of a forcing bag and a large rose pipe with the following mixture: Take 3 hard boiled yolks of eggs, a large tablespoonful of Béchamel sauce, a dust of coralline pepper, a little salt, 1 dessertspoonful of chopped chutney, a little apricot yellow, 1 tablespoonful of salad oil, 2½ ozs. fresh butter, a dessertspoonful tarragon vinegar, and either 4 washed and boned anchovies or a tablespoonful of lobster paste. Pound all together till smooth then rub through a hair sieve and use. Sprinkle over the croûtons some finely chopped parsley and dish them up en couronne on a dish on a paper and serve in the centre the following salad: Take some freshly gathered radishes, clean and cut them into square pieces, put them in cold water till crisp. Drain them, add as much fresh crisp lettuce broken small, and an equal quantity of cut cucumber, season with salt, salad oil, tarragon and chervil chopped and a little tarragon vinegar, then use.

Fillets d'Appetit Sild aux Fines Herbes

Take some appetit sild,* lay them on a plate and season them with salad oil, chopped parsley, tarragon and chervil. Serve on croûtes of fried bread with a slice of raw tomato. On each place one of the prepared fillets.

Filets de Harengs à la Jubilee

Fry some thin croûtons of bread until they are a nice golden colour. When cold place on each a fillet of herring or piece of appetit sild and by means of a forcing bag and pipe arrange some anchovy butter round it close to the edge and over the fish. Put some strips of French gherkins and hard boiled white of egg cut in thin strips. Ornament them with hard boiled yolk of egg rubbed through a wire sieve and red chillies. To make the anchovy butter, mix 2 ozs. butter, a teaspoonful of anchovy essence, half the juice of a lemon and a little of Marshall's carmine. Mix well.

Green Butter

4 anchovies well washed and pounded in a mortar. Boil some parsley and rub through a sieve with 2 ozs. fresh butter. Mix all well together and make into pats. To be eaten cold with hot crisp toast.

* Appetit sild were canned, smoked sild.

Herrings Roes à la Cairo

Cut some rounds of stale bread about 1 inch thick with a round cutter or square pieces about 3½ inches long by 1 inch deep. Make an inner cutting in the centre of each and fry them till a pale golden colour. When cooked remove the crumb from the centre cutting and place in the spaces thus formed a slice of tomato prepared as follows: Cut the raw ripe tomatoes into thin slices, season with salt, coralline pepper, a tiny piece of chopped shallot and raw green parsley. Cook for about 6 or 7 minutes in a buttered sautépan with a buttered paper over and use. Place on the tomato a piece of cooked herring roe (either from the tinned roes or fresh roes put into salt water and a little lemon juice. Bring to the boil, drain and use) and fill up the space with the cheese cream prepared as follows: Put into a stewpan 4 ozs. finely diced Gruyère or Cheddar cheese, 2 tablespoonfuls of thick Béchamel sauce, a gill of cream and a little pepper. Stir till boiling then use at once. Quickly brown the croûtons with a salamander,* dish up on a hot dish on a paper and serve as a savoury.

Kluskies au Fromage

Take 4 ozs. good Cheddar cheese cut into slices and put in a stewpan with 2 large tablespoonfuls of thick cream. Stir on the fire till melted and smooth, season with

* A salamander was a metal instrument made red-hot in the fire and then held over a food to brown it. The part heated consisted of a thick plate of iron and sometimes there was a stand to hold it. An iron fire shovel made an improvised salamander.

pepper and salt. Add 2 ozs. white bread-crumbs, 2 ozs. warm butter, 2 raw yolks and 1 white of egg that have been stirred till quite creamy. Mix well together and leave till set. Divide and roll into balls or cylinders with a little fine flour and fry or poach as liked. If fried, egg and crumb them, if poached drop into boiling milk and water and poach for 4½ minutes, drain on a sieve and dish up. Pour round some black butter or tomato butter. *Black butter:* Put into a frying pan 2 ozs. fresh butter and brown on the fire, throw into the pan some chopped raw parsley and pour over the shapes, then put in the same pan 2 tablespoonfuls of French vinegar, boil it up and pour over the butter and parsley. *Tomato butter:* Put 2 or 3 tomatoes into a stewpan with 2 ozs. butter, ¼ pint light gravy, the juice of half a lemon and ⅛ of an oz. of arrowroot that is mixed with 1 tablespoonful of cold gravy. Season with a little salt and pepper, add a little carmine and simmer on the side of the stove for 15 to 20 minutes. Rub through a tammy, rewarm and use.

Lax au Concombre

Peel a cucumber very carefully and evenly leaving pieces of the peel on at intervals, forming stripes of green and white, the white being three times the width of the green. Cut into lengths of 1½ inches, scoop out as much as possible of the pulp from one end leaving only the thinnest sides and some of the other end as a bottom to form little cups. Drain the water from the pulp, season it with oil, vinegar, pepper and salt. Fill the cups with the mixture till piled above the sides. Sprinkle with some finely chopped parsley. Take some slices of bread and butter, cut out with a round fancy cutter. Cut with the same cutter some lax* to place on the bread and butter. On the centre place the cucumber cups, garnish with some sprigs of chervil and cress. Dish on a lace dish paper. Tomato pulp (fresh tomatoes) can be used in the cucumber cups either with the cucumber pulp or alone.

Lax Canapés

Cut some slices of stale bread ¼ inch thick, cut into rounds or any fancy shape. Fry in butter till lightly browned. When cold spread anchovy butter over them and lay on the butter thin slices of lax.† Smoked salmon or cod's roe may be used.

Little Soufflés of Luxette

Take for 5 or 6 soufflés 1 jar of luxette,‡ put into a basin with 1½ gills of good fish gravy in which ¼ oz. leaf gelatine has been dissolved. Add a few drops carmine and a little coralline pepper. When smooth add ½ pint whipped cream, stir together and put the mixture into

* Lax was canned, smoked salmon cutlets preserved in oil and imported from Norway.

† Lax, *see* previous recipe.

‡ Annie says luxette 'came in a bottle like anchovy sauce—it was very thick and light brown in colour and we never used much of it at a time.'

The Army and Navy Stores catalogue of 1907 lists it as 'Luxette. Marshall's Terrine, 1/- a jar.'

a forcing bag with plain pipe and fill some little soufflé cases that have been surrounded with bands of plain paper standing about 1½ inches above the cases. Set them in a cold place for about 1 hour, then remove the paper bands and sprinkle the soufflés with a little coralline pepper. Place them on a dish with a paper and garnish with watercress.

Little Victoria Salads

Cut some new brown tin bread into thin slices, spread one side of each with butter and luxette.* Roll them up into a cylinder shape with a little well washed watercress or mustard and cress in the centre. Sprinkle over with a little lobster coral or coralline pepper. Stand each upright in a little ring of cucumber (raw), then arrange on the top of each a farced† olive and a scalloped radish. Serve out to each person on a separate plate for a savoury or hors d'oeuvre.

Luxette Biscuits

Make some cheese paste as if for cheese straws, roll it out and cut into rounds with a fluted cutter, prick well and bake in a quick oven. When cold spread them with a layer of luxette paste.‡ Place a farced olive in the middle of each and with a forcing bag and small pipe ornament the edges of the biscuits with green butter.

* Luxette, *see* previous recipe.
† A stuffed olive.
‡ Luxette, *see* Little Soufflés of Luxette, page 94.

Oval Eggs

Boil 6 eggs hard. Cut them in half lengthways, take out the yolks and pound them in a mortar with 1 tablespoonful of chicken and ham mixed, 1 teaspoonful of chopped parsley, pepper and salt to taste and a very small piece of onion chopped very fine and a small piece of butter melted. Mix all well together and fill the hollow in the white with it. Join the other half to fit it and rub the outside with flour. Cover with egg, roll in bread-crumbs and fry a pale brown colour.

Oyster and Mushroom Savoury

Fry some round croûtons of bread till a pale golden colour. On these spread some anchovy butter, arrange on each a well cooked mushroom and in the centre of each mushroom place a boiled oyster. Have some very nice white sauce made with cream and pour a spoonful over each oyster. Serve very hot.

Parmesan Pyramids

Make some round cheese biscuits out of the same paste as cheese straws. Bake them and when cold place on a dish. Whip some cream to a stiff froth, flavour lightly with Parmesan cheese, cayenne and white pepper and salt. Pile up on each biscuit and serve. If liked strips of anchovy may be placed on the cream.

Pastry à la Greville

With a fluted cutter stamp out some rounds of puff paste, egg them and bake in a quick oven for 20 minutes, let them get cold. Fill some bouché moulds with the following mixture: Take ½ pint liquid aspic jelly, add to it 2 ozs. grated Gruyère or Cheddar cheese, ½ oz. grated Parmesan, ½ oz. lean chopped cooked ham, a teaspoonful chopped parsley, a saltspoonful French mustard, a pinch of salt and a saltspoonful of Chilli vinegar. Mix together with a ¼ pint stiffly whipped cream. Pour into the bouché shapes. When set turn out and arrange a bouché shape on each round of paste and with a forcing bag and rose pipe garnish the top with savoury cream and place in the centre of this a farced olive. Arrange on a dish on small papers and serve for a second course dish. Savoury cream is prepared by taking ¼ pint stiffly whipped cream, add to it a pinch of salt and a dust of coralline pepper. Then add a few drops of carmine and use.

Petites Croûtades au Luxette

Take some boat shaped moulds and line them thinly with some savoury biscuit paste. Trim the edges and prick the bottoms of the paste to prevent blistering and bake till a pretty fawn colour. Then garnish the edges with a little plain butter and sprinkle the butter with a little chopped parsley. Take the contents of a jar of Luxette,*

* Annie says Luxette 'came in a bottle like anchovy sauce—it was very thick and light brown in colour and we never used much of it at a time.'

The Army and Navy Stores catalogue of 1907 lists it as 'Luxette. Marshall's Terrine, 1/- a jar.'

add the yolks of 2 hard boiled eggs, a little butter, coralline pepper and a few drops of carmine. Pass through a sieve then put into a forcing bag with a large rose pipe and force into the Croûtades.

Sardines à la Cambridge

Take 6 sardines, remove the skin and back bone. Rub through a fine hair sieve. Mix them with 3 minced raw bearded oysters, 1 hard-boiled yolk of egg, a tiny bit of cayenne pepper, 1½ ozs. freshly made white bread-crumbs, 1 oz. warm butter, the liquor from the oysters and 1 raw yolk of egg. Divide the mixture into portions about the size of a Spanish nut, roll in flour. Dip into beaten whole egg, then into fine white bread-crumbs and put into a frying basket. Fry for 3 or 4 minutes in boiling fat. Dish up in a pile on a hot dish with a dish paper and serve at once. Garnish with fresh parsley. A hot savoury.

Savoury à la Burghfield

Cut some slices of brown bread about ¾ inch thick, spread them with lobster paste or anchovy butter. Cut into squares, rounds or oblong pieces. Arrange some slices of lax* to completely cover the butter, ornament with alternate stripes of pink and green butter.

* Lax was canned smoked salmon cutlets preserved in oil.

Stuffed Eggs

Boil 4 eggs quite hard (15 minutes). Shell them and cut a small piece off each end of white. Halve them and remove yolks and whilst hot put them in a basin with 1 oz. butter, 1 teaspoonful anchovy, one ditto Worcester sauce, a little parsley and a few chives chopped. Mix well together and rub through a sieve. Fill in the cases of white with the feathery mixture, *do not smooth or Flatten.* Serve on a dish paper with well washed and drained lettuce round.

Soufflés

Little Soufflés à la Marlborough

Mix together 1 tablespoonful of fine flour, 2 ozs. castor sugar, 2 tablespoonfuls of desiccated coconut with a ¼ pint thick cream. Pour on to this ¼ pint boiling cream, pour all into a pan and boil carefully. Place aside till cool. Rub the contents of a small jar of orange marmalade through a coarse sieve. Beat the yolks and whites of 3 eggs separately, stir the marmalade pulp into the first mixture then add the eggs. Pour into little china soufflé cases. Bake in a moderate oven about 10 minutes. Sprinkle with pink sugar and serve. You can put lemon marmalade or apricot jam if preferred.

Lobster Soufflés

Put in a saucepan 3 ozs. flour and 3 ozs. of butter. Mix over the fire till the butter has taken up the flour, add 1½ pints of milk and stir till it thickens. Set aside half to make sauce for the soufflé and to the other half add ¾ tin of lobster cut small, or the meat of a small fresh boiled lobster. A bit of coral pounded with ½ oz. butter may be added. Put salt and pepper to taste, 1 tablespoonful of anchovy sauce, 1 dessertspoonful of vinegar, 1 tablespoonful of Worcester sauce. Mix all together and add the beaten yolks of 4 eggs and the whites of 6 eggs beaten to a stiff froth. Tie a band of buttered paper round a well buttered mould and steam 1¼ hours. The tin must be filled half full. *For the sauce:* Put into a saucepan the sauce reserved, some milk to make it the right consistency and pepper and salt to taste. Boil up and add some of the lobster coral pounded and a tablespoonful of anchovy sauce. When the soufflé is ready turn it out and pour the sauce round. Serve very hot.

Soufflé of Dried Haddock

Remove all the skin and bone from a good sized dried haddock and rub the fish through a wire sieve. Put the skin and bones into a stewpan with 1 or 2 sliced onions and a bunch of herbs and cover them with milk. Add a few peppercorns and a teaspoonful of anchovy essence. Place the pan on the stove and let the milk simmer for ½ an hour, then strain into a basin. Take 3 ozs. butter and the same quantity of flour (Vienna),* a little salt and cayenne pepper, 2 teaspoonfuls of anchovy essence and 4 raw yolks of eggs. Mix these together and add by degrees ¾ pint of the milk in which the haddock bones were boiled. Stir over the fire till it boils taking care that it is quite smooth and free from lumps, then add a very little cold milk and the haddock that has been rubbed through the sieve. Lastly add the stiffly whipped whites of 6 eggs and stir the mixture as lightly as possible when adding these. Well butter a soufflé tin and fasten a band of well buttered paper round it so that it will stand about 4 or 5 inches above the edge of the tin. Pour in the mixture and sprinkle some browned crumbs over the top and place small pieces of butter here and there. Bake the soufflé in a fairly hot oven for ¾ of an hour. When cooked remove the band of paper, place a

* Vienna flour—a strong fine white flour.

folded napkin round the tin and sprinkle a little finely chopped parsley over the top.

Strawberry Soufflé

Take 3 gills of fresh ripe strawberries, rub the fruit through a fine hair sieve. Put into a stewpan 2½ ozs. Vienna flour,* 2 ozs. fresh butter, 1 gill cream or milk, ¾ lb. castor sugar, a few drops of essence of vanilla and enough carmine or cochineal to make the mixture a pretty pink. Finally add the raw yolks of 4 eggs. The strawberry pulp must be added to the above ingredients and all together should be stirred over the fire till it boils. Then add about a tablespoonful of milk to stop the mixture cooking. To the mixture add rather more than ½ lb. of strawberries that have been sliced and lastly add the stiffly whipped whites of 6 eggs. Pour into the soufflé tin, prepared as in the previous receipt and sprinkle over the top a little icing sugar and after the soufflé has been cooking about ¼ hour again sprinkle it with icing sugar. For the sauce: Pound 1 lb. strawberries, ½ lb. castor sugar, the juice of a lemon and a little carmine or cochineal. Rub through a fine hair sieve, then ice before serving.

* Vienna flour, *see* previous recipe.

Soups

Consommé à la Cirque

Put 2 tablespoonfuls of crême de volaille in a paper cornet, and press it into tiny rounds on a buttered baking sheet. Place a pea-shaped piece of cooked carrot in the centre of each, cover them with a buttered paper. Moisten them with a little consommé, and cook them in a moderately heated oven. Drain the circles on a cloth, and put them with picked chervil leaves in good clear soup.

Friar Tuck Soup

First make a nice white stock with either veal, rabbit or chicken and flavour it well with vegetables. Put into a stewpan and bring it to boiling point. Cut a nice young chicken into joints and add to the soup together with 2 leeks which have been cut into fine shreds and blanched. Cook in about 1½ ozs. butter for 20 minutes but do not allow them to brown. Add one handful fresh parsley and same amount of chervil. Let the soup cook for ½ an hour then take the chicken from it and keep it warm between two plates over boiling water. Whip 4 eggs and add these to the soup but do not allow it to boil or it will curdle. Stir it till it becomes creamy then add the meat from the chicken cut in dice and quite free from skin and bone. Season with a little salt and mignonette pepper.* Hand fried croûtons with the soup.

* Mignonette pepper—coarsely ground white peppercorns.

Oyster Soup

Season 1 pint cream and 1 pint white stock with pepper and salt and a tiny pinch of mace. Add 3 ozs. butter rolled in flour. Bring to the boil and let it simmer for 5 minutes. Have one score of oysters bearded, put them in the soup tureen, add the liquor from them to the boiling soup. Pour over the oysters in the tureen and serve.

Sweets

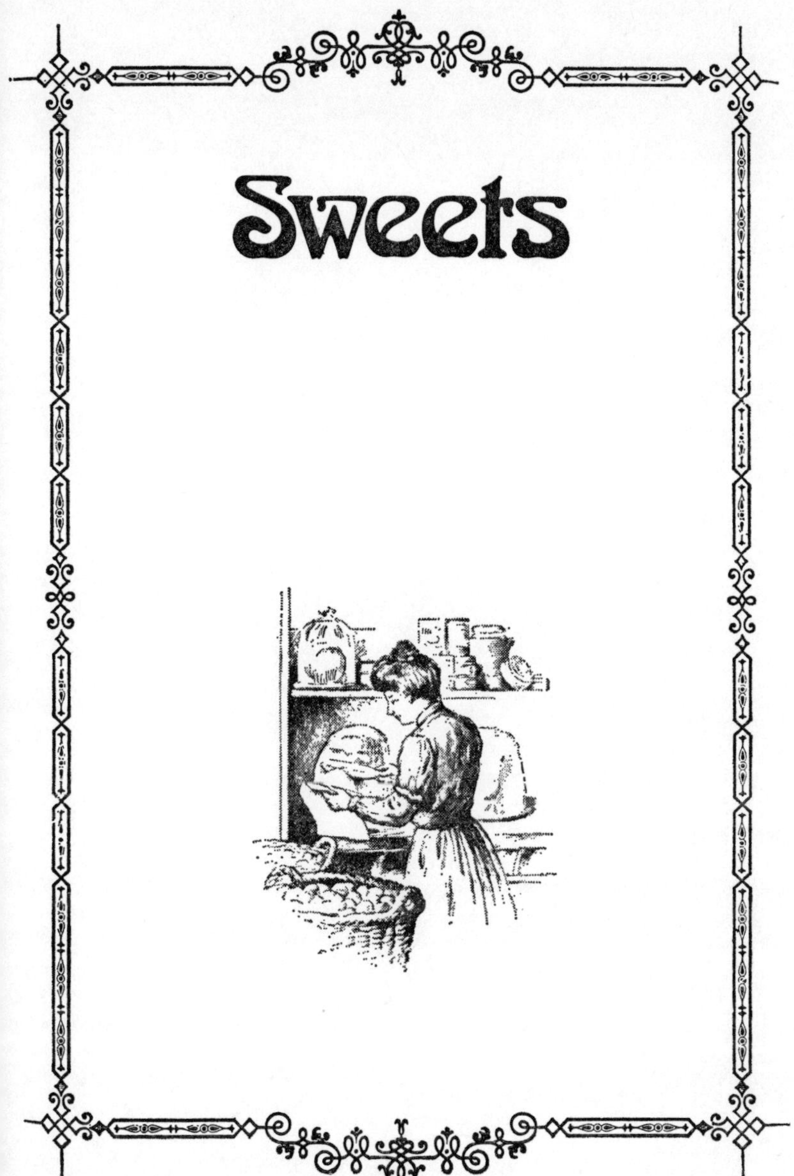

Apple Cheesecakes

3 ozs. apple grated, 3 ozs. butter melted, 3 ozs. castor sugar, the rind of a lemon grated and a small quantity of the juice. 3 eggs, one white left out. Mix well, line some patty pans with puff paste, put in the mixture and bake.

Apples à la Frangipane

Peel and core 12 apples. Stew them and slice them into a deep dish and shake some castor sugar over. Spread apricot jam thinly over and very thin slices of fresh butter over the jam. Take 1 oz. of arrowroot and mix it with 1 pint cream, a small bit of butter and sugar enough to sweeten it. Stir it over the fire till it begins to boil then lay it over the apples and bake in a moderate oven.

Bavaroise à la Princess of Wales

Line a fancy mould thinly with clear lemon jelly (see page 50) and arrange at the top of the shape some pieces of chocolate Bavaroise and some pink and white lemon cream. Set them to the shape with a little more jelly then line the remainder of the mould with gold and silver leaf* jelly flavoured with Maraschino or any other liquor. When this is set line the shape all over with pink lemon cream and fill up the centre with orange cream and Maraschino cream in alternate layers. When the shape is full put aside till cold then turn out on to a dish on to a paper. *Orange cream:* Take 3 large oranges and rub thin slices on 3 ozs. loaf sugar. Put the sugar into a basin and add the strained juice of the oranges and a tablespoonful of apricot jam, a saltspoonful of apricot yellow, 6 drops of almond essence and a small glass of Curaçoa. Add to this ¾ pint strong lemon jelly made by reducing 1½ pints, rub through the tammy. When cool add a gill of cream and ½ wineglassful of Kirsch liquor and use. *Maraschino cream:* Take ½ pint strong lemon jelly, mix with it 1½ gills whipped cream, 1 large wineglassful of Maraschino and ½ wineglassful of brandy and use. *Chocolate Bavaroise:* Put into a stewpan 2 ozs. grated chocolate with ½ pint water, 2 ozs. icing sugar and the peel of a lemon. Let it simmer for 15 minutes then rub through a tammy. Add 1 teaspoonful of vanilla essence, ½ wineglassful of Maraschino and when cooling pour into a tin or flat dish and leave till cold. Then stamp out with a leaf cutter and use. *Lemon cream:* Take 1 pint strong lemon jelly, mix with it 1½ gills thick cream, flavour with a small glass of Curaçoa or Maraschino, tammy, divide into two pastes, colour one with carmine and leave the other plain, then use as instructed.

* Alexis Soyer in his book *The Modern Housewife* says that 'gold or silver leaf jelly is made with *eau de vie de Dantzic* mixing the gold and silver leaves with a little jelly. It can also be made by cutting up a quarter of a sheet of gold leaf in a glass of pale brandy, and use in this form.'

Eau de vie de Dantzic was a German liqueur, *Danziger goldwasser.*

Charlotte à l'Italienne

Whisk the white of 4 eggs to a stiff froth, mix in 8 ozs. of finely-pounded icing sugar mixed together. Press the meringue through a tube on to an oiled baking-sheet, dust with sugar, and dry in a cool oven. When they are done and cold, mask the oval part alternately with coffee and white icing, and when they are dry arrange them in an upright position in a plain mould, that is lined with oiled paper, using a little icing to stick them together. Next day turn the charlotte on to a round piece of Genoese cake, fixing it with a little icing, and, when it is firm, fill the charlotte with a good cream Bavaroise, which can be made in this way: Mash 1 lb. of ripe raspberries or strawberries with 6 ozs. of sugar; allow them to stand for an hour, then rub them through a hair sieve. Mix the purée with half a pint of cream and ½ oz. of dissolved gelatine. Put the cream in the charlotte when it is on the point of setting, making it look as rocky as possible.

Chartreuse of Oranges

Peel 3 oranges and 1 lemon *very* thinly; put the rind into a stewpan with ½ lb. loaf sugar, a little cinnamon, 1 or 2 cloves, a little saffron yellow, 1½ ozs. of gelatine, 1 quart cold water and the juice of the oranges (3) and lemon (1) and the whites and shells of 2 eggs. Mix all together with a whisk and place the pan on the stove; bring gently to boiling point stirring from time to time with the whisk before it comes to the boil. Draw the pan to the side of the fire and let it remain 10 minutes; strain through the jelly bag. When the jelly has cooled line a plain charlotte mould with it to the thickness of ½ an inch, ornament the mould with quarters of orange freed from all white pith and skin and pips and with glacé cherries cut in strips and mixed with a little of the jelly coloured with carmine. Arrange some of the divisions of orange in a circle at the bottom of the mould and in the centre place some of the cherries in jelly which has quite set. Set the ornamentation with some of the same jelly that the mould was *lined* with and proceed to arrange the divisions of orange round the sides ornamenting with the cherries. When the mould is finished make a Bavaroise in the following way: Put into a saucepan ¾ pint milk and a split vanilla pod, bring the milk slowly to boiling point then draw the pan to the side of the stove and let it remain for ½ an hour, then add 3¼ ozs. castor sugar, ½ oz. gelatine and when the gelatine and sugar have dissolved pour it on the well beaten yolks of 3 eggs. Return the custard to the saucepan and stir it over the fire till it thickens but on no account allow it to boil. Set it aside till cool; flavour the custard with pineapple syrup and add ½ pint whipped cream and stir *very* lightly. Pour into the mould and let it set. When you wish to serve dip the mould into warm water, then turn out on to a clean cloth to absorb all moisture and remove carefully into the dish it is to be served in.

Compote of Oranges

Peel the fruit *very* thinly, taking care not to remove any white pith with the rind. Add the rind to a syrup made by boiling ½ lb. of loaf sugar with a gill of water till reduced to a thick syrup. Boil the rind in the syrup for 5 or 6 minutes. Remove all the white pith and skin from the oranges and divide them into thin natural divisions. Place the fruit in a pile on a dish and pour a little brandy over the fruit. Strain the syrup through muslin over the fruit.

Éclairs à la Vanderbilt

Put into a stewpan ½ pint water, 4 ozs. butter and 2 ozs. castor sugar. Bring to the boil then mix into it 5 ozs. fine flour that has been rubbed through a sieve. Stir well together and stand on the stove to cook for 10 minutes. Then remove from stove and let the mixture cool. Then mix in by degrees 3 whole eggs and 6 or 8 drops vanilla essence. Put this paste into a forcing bag with a large plain pipe, force it out on to a baking tin in lengths of 4 inches by ½ an inch. Cover the paste with a pastry cover* and bake in a moderate oven for about 15 to 20 minutes. Then take up and when cold split down the side and with a forcing bag and plain pipe fill them with the following: Take ½ pint new

* A pastry cover was used by commercial confectioners. It was a special tin cover but a bread or similar tin made an adequate substitute. Choux pastry was supposed to rise better under such a cover; but these are seldom used in modern thermostatically controlled ovens.

milk and boil it with 3 ozs. castor sugar and the finely cut peel of 2 oranges and 2 lemons. Simmer for about ten minutes then dissolve in the mixture rather more than ¼ oz. leaf gelatine and stir on to 3 yolks of eggs (raw). Mix together on the fire till the custard thickens, colour with a little apricot yellow and rub through a sieve. When cool add ¼ pint strained orange and lemon juice, a teaspoonful of vanilla essence and ¼ pint whipped cream and a tablespoonful of any liqueur. Stir on ice till setting then use. After filling the pastry cases put on a pastry rack or sieve and glaze in three divisions with pink, white and brown glacés prepared as follows; and then when set arrange on a dish paper and serve. *Pink and white glacé:* ¾ lb. icing sugar, 2½ tablespoonfuls of any liqueur and the same quantity of water. Stir well together then divide into two parts. Colour one with carmine, leaving the other plain. Just warm them and use. *Brown glacé:* 6 ozs. icing sugar, 1 dessertspoonful coffee essence and sufficient water to make a thick batter when it is ready to use. Decorate the éclairs thus.

Gâteau aux Fruits

Beat 2 ozs. of butter with 2 ozs. of pounded sugar until it is white, add an egg, and then 3 ozs. of flour mixed with a saltspoonful of baking powder; put it into a well-greased border mould and bake it in a moderate oven about half an hour. Serve it with plain stewed fruit of any kind in the middle and round it, and garnish it with a little whipped cream on the top.

Golden Crown Tartlets

These tartlets are simple and pretty:

To make them, rub 4 ozs. of butter into 6 ozs. of flour, make a well and put in 2 ozs. of sugar, the yolk of an egg and a teaspoonful of water. Work it into a paste. Line the tartlet tins with the paste, brush them over with beaten egg, prick them well with a fork, and bake them a delicate colour, in a moderate oven. Allow them to cool, before removing them from the tins. Open a tin of peaches and boil them down with the syrup, adding a little brandy. When they are cold, place half a peach in each tartlet, with a spoonful of the reduced syrup. Pipe them round the edge with some whipped cream, sprinkle them lightly with chopped pistachios, and arrange them on a dessert paper.

Little Baskets à la Pauline

Well oil some fluted basket moulds then line them thinly with the following: Put ½ lb. almonds into a saucepan, cover them with water and bring to the boil. Wash them in cold water, remove the skins, split the almonds in fine shreds, put them on a baking sheet and bake a pale brown, keeping them well turned and moved. Put ½ lb. castor sugar into a stewpan with 2 tablespoonfuls of lemon juice, boil together till a pretty golden colour. Then mix in ½ lb. of the prepared almonds, just boil up and mould the baskets. When cool turn out and stick the two parts of the baskets together with some boiled sugar. Fill them with stiffly whipped cream sweetened and flavoured with vanilla essence and coloured with carmine. Garnish with strips of angelica, crystallized violets or any other pretty garnish. Arrange the baskets on a dish on a paper and surround with spun sugar.

Orange Snow

Dissolve ½ oz. gelatine in water, add ½ lb. loaf sugar and the juice of 4 oranges and the rind grated. Boil for 10 minutes. Strain and when cold add the whites of 2 eggs well beaten, whisk all together till light and like snow. Then either pour into a mould to set or pile high in a glass dish.

Stewed Pears

Put them into a tin lined pan, cover them with some sugar and water mixed and 2 or 3 cloves. Let them boil fast for 2 or 3 hours till tender. When done enough squeeze into them the juice of a lemon and cover till cold.

Suprême de Pêches

Set a little clear jelly garnished with pistachios in a cylinder mould, and arrange quarters of good, ripe peaches around the sides of the mould, setting each layer with jelly and chopped pistachios. Meanwhile, pound 4 or 5 ripe peaches, and rub them through a hair sieve, mix the purée with a gill of syrup, flavoured with the peach kernels and a little Noyeau. Add a tablespoonful of lemon juice, and freeze it in the ice machine. When ready to serve, turn the mould on to a dish, and fill the centre with the prepared ice. Serve it very quickly.

Vanilla Timbale with Fruits

Put into a stewpan ½ pint new milk, 2 ozs. castor sugar, a vanilla pod and the peel of one lemon. Bring to the boil and let it infuse for ¼ hour. Dissolve in it ½ oz. gelatine (leaf). Mix into it 3 raw yolks of eggs and stir over the fire till it thickens, it *must not* boil. Then rub through a sieve and when *cool* add ½ pint stiffly whipped cream and a wineglassful of orange flower water. Then pour into a timbale or turban mould. When cold turn out and fill up the centre with compote of fruits or a macedoine prepared as follows: Take any ripe fruit (strawberries, grapes, cherries stoned, bananas, pineapple sliced, currants, raspberries etc.). Mix them with some castor sugar and a few drops of carmine, sprinkle them with Maraschino, Noyeau or Kirsch and keep on ice till wanted.

Venetian Apples

Take 2½ lbs. of peeled and finely sliced cooking apples, the *finely* peeled and chopped rind of 2 lemons and the strained juice. 1 jar greengage jam, 4 bay leaves, ½ lb. castor sugar and ¼ pint water. Put them into a stewpan with 1 oz. fresh butter and a few drops of carmine, simmer till tender. Mix with ½ oz. of Marshall's leaf gelatine and when dissolved run through a hair sieve. Set aside till cold then arrange in a pile in a deep glass dish and garnish round with little leaf shapes of puff paste prepared as follows and between the leaves put small roses of whipped cream sweetened and flavoured with vanilla and coloured with carmine. *Leaf shapes of paste for garnishing:* Take some puff paste, roll out thinly, cut into leaf shapes, brush over with raw beaten egg and bake till a nice golden colour. When cold glaze with Maraschino glacé, sprinkle with chopped pistachio nuts or little assorted sweets. *Maraschino glacé:* Take ¾ lb. icing sugar, add a little sap green, Maraschino liqueur to taste making the mixture the thickness of cream. Stir on the fire till warm then use.

Various

Biscuit Paste

1 lb. flour, 4 ozs. butter, 1 oz. sugar, 1 egg well beaten and a small quantity of milk all mixed up together.

Black Puddings

Catch the blood of a hog. To each quart of blood put a large teaspoonful of salt, and stir it without ceasing, till it is cold. Simmer half a pint of Emden groats* till tender in a little water—there must be no gruel. Chop up (for one quart of blood) 1 lb. of the inside fat of the hog, a quarter of a pint of bread-crumbs, tablespoonful of sage, chopped fine, teaspoonful of thyme, 3 drachms of allspice, salt, and pepper, and a teacupful of cream. When the blood is cold, strain it through a sieve, and add it to the fat, then the groat and seasoning. Well mix, put it into the largest guts, well cleansed, tie it into lengths of about nine inches, and boil gently for twenty minutes. Take them out and prick them when they have boiled a few minutes.

* Emden groats were the best quality groats. Annie says she, in fact, used the coarser kind of oatmeal so that 'the white pieces showed'—in the White Puddings ordinary oatmeal was used.

Cream of Nectar

To 4 lbs. lump sugar put 6 quarts cold water. Stir and set over a slow fire till it is milk warm. Add the well beaten whites of 2 eggs. Bring the whole to nearly boiling point, let it just boil and strain immediately. When cold add 6 ozs. tartaric acid, ½ tablespoonful carbonate of soda and flavour to taste with essence of lemon. Bottle for use and when wanted take a wineglassful in a tumbler of water. A wineglassful of sherry is a great improvement.

Faggots

1½ lbs. pig's liver, ½ lb. fat pork, a teaspoonful each of sage, parsley and thyme (powdered), a good sized onion, ½ pint bread-crumbs, two eggs, a teaspoonful of pepper and double the quantity of salt, a pinch of grated nutmeg, and a pig's caul. The meat must be very finely minced, and mixed with the seasoning, then put in a jar and steamed in a saucepan with boiling water halfway round it, for an hour. It must then be left to cool before mixing with the bread-crumbs and eggs. After beating well, make the mass into balls, and flatten a little, wrap them singly in pieces of the caul, and bake gently to a pale brown, about half an hour. The onion should be scalded and chopped, if a mild flavour is desired, otherwise it can be put in raw, and in rather larger pieces.

Game Pie

Cut the breasts or fillets and the legs off two or three birds, sprinkle them with pepper and salt, and cook them in the oven, smothered with butter. Pound the carcases, and make of them some good gravy, but do not thicken it. Take the livers of the birds with an equal quantity of calf's liver, mince both, and toss them in butter over the fire for a minute or two; then pound them in a mortar with an equal quantity of bacon, two shallots, parboiled, with pepper, salt, powdered spice, and sweet herbs to taste. When this mixture is well pounded, pass it through a sieve. Put a layer of this forcemeat into a piedish, arrange the pieces of partridge, or any other game, filling up the interstices with the forcemeat. Then pour in as much gravy as is required, put on the cover of paste, which should be made as follows: Sift 2 lbs. of fine flour to one and a half of good salt butter, break it into small pieces, and wash it well in cold water; rub gently together the butter and flour, and mix it up with the yolks of three eggs, beat together with a spoon, a pint of spring water. Roll it out, and double it into folds three times, and it is ready. Bake for an hour. Half the quantity can be made according to size of pie. When done a little more gravy may be added through the hole in the centre of the pie.

Ginger Beer

4 lemons, 4 lbs. lump sugar, ¼ lb. whole ginger bruised, 4 ozs. cream of tartar. Pour 4 gallons boiling water on the

above and when cold add a little yeast on toast. Let it work 12 hours then bottle. It will be ready to drink in two days after being bottled.

Gunter's Sandwiches

Pound the yolk of a hard boiled egg very smooth with a good large piece of butter, a teaspoonful of Worcester sauce, the same of Anchovy and a few drops of vinegar, a large pinch of *dry* mustard. Spread this on slices of bread, cover with finely chopped mustard and cress and if liked a little minced chicken and ham. Sprinkle with the chopped white of the egg and cover with another slice of bread spread with the mixture. Cut into squares, rounds or triangles with a very sharp knife, after removing all the crust.

Hunter's Beef

Sprinkle the beef with salt and after 2 days let it drain, then put it in the pickle which must be made as follows: To 8 gallons water put 8 lbs. Bay salt,* 8 lbs. common salt, 1 lb. brown sugar and 1 lb. saltpetre. When well boiled and cold, put it on the beef. There should sometimes be a few lbs. of salt put into the cask to keep the pickle strong. The beef will be fit for use in 10 days or a fortnight.

* Bay salt. At this period there were six different methods used for producing salt. Bay salt was the most expensive but said to have the best flavour. It was obtained by the evaporation of sea-water and was generally coarser than other salt.

Mincemeat (1)

1 lb. suet, 1 lb. sultanas, 1 lb. apples, 1 lb. currants, ½ lb. candied peel, 1 lb. sugar, grated rind and juice of 2 lemons. Chop all fine and mix with one glass of brandy and ¼ nutmeg grated (if liked).

Mincemeat (2)

1 lb. currants, 1 lb. sultanas, 1 lb. beef suet, 1 lb. brown sugar, ¼ lb. orange peel, ¼ lb. lemon peel, ¼ lb. citron, 1 lb. apples, juice of 2 lemons, the rind of 1 grated, ½ nutmeg grated, 1 teaspoonful pounded mace. Chop up all the ingredients as fine as possible and mix well together with a gill of brandy.

Pikelets

1 quart warm milk, 2 eggs, little salt, little sugar, ½d. yeast, then mix in flour sauce as pancakes. Let them stand 1½ hours, then bake. A little baking powder just before baking makes them lighter.

Pork Sausages

3½ lbs. fat, 5 lbs. ham of pork, 1½ ozs. ground white pepper, 1 oz. salt, 2 nutmegs grated and 1 loaf, 2d. size.*

* Annie says a loaf, 2d. size, was a small tin loaf.

Cut the loaf into pieces and soak in cold water till soft. Squeeze the water from the bread and mix the bread with the fat and ham of pork which must have been freed from all bone, gristle and skin and cut up into pieces about 2 inches square. Add the salt, pepper, nutmeg and any herbs that may be liked, whilst mixing. Pass all through the mincing machine. Have the skins thoroughly cleaned and soaked for 10 minutes in cold water. Push the skin on to the pipe of the machine till the length is all on the pipe (previously wet the pipe to make the skin work on properly) then fill the machine with mixture and force it into the skins, passing the skins through the thumb and finger as they are filling to make them the same size all along. When filled take a length, divide it (not cut it) twist it then twist each side at intervals passing one side through the other at the twist to make the sausages.

Quails à la Souvaroff

Bone as many quails as are required and cut them into quarters. Place them in a Souvaroff Jar closely together and on the top put a layer of sliced truffles (fresh ones are *much* the best), then another layer of birds and cover the top with more truffles, then entirely cover with Sherry. Make a paste with a little white of egg and flour and colour it with a little saffron yellow. With this fasten up the small hole in the lid, place the lid on the jar. Then take a strip of foolscap paper about an inch wide spread some of the paste on it and arrange it round the jar so that no air can get in where the lid ends. Place the jar in a tin containing sufficient hot water to come three parts of the way up the jar, put into a moderate oven and cook for ½ an hour. If this dish is going to be served cold the lid should not be removed until it is served, and even when served hot the lid should not be removed till in the dining room.

Sandwiches

Pound together 2 ozs. butter and 1 oz. Parmesan cheese. When quite smooth add ½ teaspoonful Worcester sauce and same quantity anchovy and if liked a small spoonful (tea) of finely chopped chives. Cut some slices of bread, spread them with the mixture and on it lay thin slices of tongue, beef, mutton, ham or any sliced meat, nicely freed from all skin and gristle. Cover with another slice of bread spread with the mixture and cut into neat squares or triangles, after removing all the crust.

Sandwiches à la Portugaise

Take some thinly cut slices of bread and butter, mask each piece lightly with French and English mustard. Sprinkle with salt and coralline pepper. Take some finely cut slices of good Cheddar spread a layer of clotted cream and on this sprinkle some chopped cooked lobster, fresh raw chopped tarragon and chervil, a little anchovy essence, and place here and there some boned filleted anchovies. Close up the bread in the usual way, pressing it well together, then cut it into square pieces or stamp out with a round cutter. Dish up the sandwiches en couronne on a dish on a paper and fill up the centre with any nice salad.

Sandwiches with Mushroom Purée

Take a stale small tin brown loaf* and cut some thin buttered slices. Sprinkle the butter side with some finely chopped cooked chicken, spread on this a layer of mushroom purée about ½ inch thick, prepared as follows: Take 6 or 8 large mushrooms chopped fine, season with salt and pepper, a large chopped eschalot, and a teaspoonful finely chopped raw parsley. Put into a stewpan with 1½ ozs. butter and draw it down on the stove till into a pulp. Then mix with it 1 oz. fresh white breadcrumbs add 1 oz. of finely cut glaze or Liebig's Extract of Meat. Stir on the fire till boiling, then set aside till cooling and use. Cover the Sandwich with another slice of bread and butter and press well together. Mask them with aspic cream and when this has set mask over the cream with liquid aspic jelly. Put them aside till set and then when cold stamp out with a plain round cutter about 1½ inches in diameter or cut into finger lengths. Dish up on a dish paper and garnish with mustard and cress or watercress and lettuce picked into sprigs.

* Annie says a small tin loaf then cost 2d.

Savoury Éclairs

4 ozs. of Vienna flour,* 2 ozs. of butter, half a pint of water, two eggs, and one extra yolk. For the mixture: ¼ lb. of cold chicken, 2 ozs. of cold ham, 1 oz. of flour, 1 oz. of butter, one teaspoonful of parsley, a dust of nutmeg, salt and pepper. Put the flour on a baking tin in the oven for a few minutes to dry it, but do not let it get in the least brown. Then sieve and weigh it, and if it has lost weight, add a little more dried flour. Put the water and butter in a clean saucepan, and when it boils, add the flour and beat it till it is smooth, then stir it in the pan over a slow fire till you can roll it about the pan without it sticking. Let it cool. Next add one egg, beat it in well, add another, and when this is beaten in add the yolk. Take the mixture—a small piece at a time—and roll it lightly on a floured board into finger-shaped rolls as long and as thick as your first finger. Put these about two inches apart on a greased baking tin, and bake them slowly till they are quite hollow and feel very light. They should be twice their original size. When they are nearly done brush the tops over with beaten yolk of egg. Split them open on one side, and without removing the tops scoop out any soft part if there is any in them.

Melt the butter in a saucepan, stir in the flour smoothly, then add the milk, and stir it over the fire till it boils. Now put in the chopped chicken, ham and parsley. Mix them well, and season them with salt and pepper. Make the mixture hot, then fill in the cases. Arrange the éclairs in a criss-cross pile on a lace paper.

* Vienna flour was a fine, white strong flour.

To Render Lard

Cut the flay or leaf into small pieces, put it into a large clean pan. Stir with a wooden spoon whilst it melts and do not put it too far on the fire. Strew the top of the stove with dry pounded salt so that any fat that gets on to the stove cannot get alight. As the fat melts remove it carefully from the pan and pour it through a fine hair sieve. When all is melted and in a liquid state (if it has become set melt it up again) pour it through a funnel, previously fixed in the neck of the bladder by soaking the neck of the bladder in warm water. Let the bladder stand in cold water whilst being filled as this will make the skins look nice and white and prevent them from wrinkling. Tie the necks of the bladders before removing the funnel.

Water Biscuits

½ lb. flour, rub in a piece of butter as large as a walnut and mix into a firm paste with milk. Roll out *very thinly*, stamp out and bake for five minutes.

White Puddings

To every 6 lbs. groats use 6 lbs. leaf lard, chopped to about the size of a nut. The groats should be boiled for about thirty minutes in the same manner as for black puddings. Add the seasoning to the puddings while hot, and four quarts of new milk. Mix the whole thoroughly well together. Fill into skins, boil for about twenty minutes in clean water. A good seasoning for white puddings can be made by mixing from 6 ozs. to 8 ozs. of fine salt with every pound of the finest ground white pepper. No herbs must be used. Use from 6 ozs. to 8 ozs. of this seasoning to every 12 lbs. of groats. The above proportions of ingredients are for a large quantity of puddings.

Vegetables

Beetroot à la Russe

Slice 3 onions and one apple and fry in 4 ozs. butter. Rub through a hair sieve, then add a little stock and the beetroot that has been previously boiled till soft and cut in slices. Just before serving add ¼ pint thick cream and pepper and salt to taste. Make very hot and serve garnished with fried croûtons.

Cucumbers à la Velouté

Take a couple of nice cucumbers, cut them in pieces 3 inches long, divide each in halves, pare off the skin, remove the seeds and trim the corners, making them a nice oval shape. Blanch the cucumbers by boiling them in salted water for 10 minutes, then drain, and finish cooking them in nicely-seasoned stock. Then take them carefully from the braise. Make a little sauce with the liquor, season it with salt, pepper, a pinch of cayenne pepper, and a little lemon juice and, at the last moment, mix in a tablespoonful of grated Parmesan cheese, and add the cucumbers to warm.

Fry a sufficient number of strips of bread in butter, drain them, and arrange a piece of cucumber on each croûte. Pour the sauce round, and sprinkle them with coralline pepper and chopped parsley.

French Beans and Cream

Take 1½ lbs. beans, string them and cut them into dice shapes. Rinse them in cold water, then cook them in a saucepan with plenty of boiling water seasoned with salt. Let the beans cook fast for ¼ hour or till tender, then strain the water from them and rinse and drain them. Chop an onion very small, put it into a pan of cold water and add a little salt, bring the water quickly to the boil and strain it from the onion. Put into a sauté pan 2 ozs. butter, 1 teaspoonful finely chopped parsley, a little salt, a sprig of thyme and the onion. Fry them together for ¼ hour but do not let them become brown. Then add rather more than 1 gill cream and 1 oz. of butter and flour mixed together. Stir these ingredients over the fire and when the sauce boils add the beans. Should the mixture be too thick a little more cream or white stock may be added.

Japanese Artichokes

*Japanese artichokes,** or, to use the French name, *crosnes*, are a delicious little vegetable dressed in the following way:

If the crosnes are very fresh the fine skin will rub off with a little coarse salt, otherwise they must be scraped and trimmed. Simmer them for half an hour in boiling water to which a little salt and lemon juice have been added, after which strain the crosnes, put them into a

* Japanese artichokes are *Stachys tubifera*, a winter vegetable which is a native of Japan; sometimes called Chinese artichokes.

gill of Hollandaise sauce and dish them in a border of croûtons.

To make the sauce, mix a dessertspoonful of flour with an ounce of dissolved butter in a stewpan, add half a gill of consommé and a little milk. Stir it until it is boiling, then add the yolks of 2 eggs with two tablespoonfuls of thick cream, a squeeze of lemon juice, 2 drops each of tarragon and chilli vinegar and pepper and salt to taste.

Magic Pain Killer

Spirit of hartshorn, 1 oz.; olive oil, 1½ ozs.; cayenne pepper, 2 drachms; laudanum, 2 drachms; one tablespoonful of salt, and two ditto brandy. Shake well in a bottle. Rub the affected part with it, apply afterwards a rag saturated with it. It removes pains and swellings. It is a magic remedy.